Is God
In My
Top Ten?

MEDITATIONS FOR A
DEEPER LIFE IN CHRIST

Jerome Kodell, OSB

Published by The Word Among Us Press
7115 Guilford Drive, Suite 100
Frederick, Maryland 21704
wau.org

22 21 20 19 18   1 2 3 4 5

ISBN: 978-1-59325-333-2
eISBN: 978-1-59325-508-4

Cover design by Faceout

Made and printed in the United States of America

Library of Congress Control Number: 2018940910

CONTENTS

Introduction

One of my responsibilities as abbot of Subiaco Abbey in the years 1989–2015 was to produce regularly an article for our newsletter, which in the early years appeared six times a year and later became a quarterly. The style and length of these essays became popular with our readers, and I was asked to gather some of the most popular in book form (published in 2009 as *Don't Trust the Abbot*). I received an invitation from The Word Among Us Press to produce similar essays for a book that appeared as *Life Lessons from the Monastery: Love, Prayer, Calling and Commitment* in 2010.

I discovered that these short articles became a comfortable range for me, well suited for balancing the responsibilities that, during those years, did not give me long stretches of time for writing. I have continued to write them with the intention of publishing them, as I am doing now, along with a selection of the most popular articles published in our newsletter since 2009. About two-thirds of the essays in this collection are new, and one-third of them are from the newsletter.

The first article appearing here, from the Summer 2013 edition of the newsletter, gives the title to the collection. There are many ways to phrase the question about one's consistent spiritual motive and purpose, but one in particular struck a chord with our readers: "Is God in My Top Ten?" The essays in this collection explore what is involved in living with a constant desire for God as the primary motive and driving force. In one way or another, the various chapters are all about developing a prayer life, not a series of disconnected activities, regular or irregular, but, rather, about life as a prayer, in the sense of the gospel admonition to pray without ceasing.

The world around us is trying more and more to block our attention from the unseen realities at the heart of it, the life-giving sources that provide the energy, joy, and passion without which the daily round of our activities is just that, a daily drone. We are encouraged to forget about the deeper things and to be absorbed in the passing attractions. Falling into this can result in a domination by the foreground—which is constantly moving and changing and can become a tornado—with an anchor in the background of our faith, our tradition, and our creed. These short essays are offered as guides along that daily spiritual journey.

PART I

KEYS TO PRAYER

1. Is God in My Top Ten?

When a new monastic applicant arrived at the monastery, St. Benedict would admonish the abbot and the community of monks to determine whether the novice "truly seeks God." While it might have seemed obvious that seeking God would be the applicant's motivation, St. Benedict knew that there could be many other underlying reasons to seek out the monastic life: to get away from current problems, the illusion of a more carefree life, personal ambition, seeking silence, or rejoining someone who has already entered. But only one motive—to seek God—could carry the applicant through the thick and thin of monastic life. This motivation may be mixed up with several unworthy motives, such as those mentioned above, and will have to be jarred loose from him and rise to the top if the vocation is going to survive and thrive.

Even when this desire to seek God above all is very strong, it requires constant nurturing. Only by daily contact with God in prayer will God remain the most important reality in our lives. Otherwise, though God will be very important and a driving force, his importance may slip, very subtly, without our noticing it. He will be like our intimate friends of childhood or college who always remain our friends but, because of time and distance, are no longer in our consciousness every day. God may remain in our top ten but no longer be the main focus of our day-to-day living. God may remain very important, but other things have a way of becoming more important than God.

When this happens, we don't make our decisions in the light of the absolute primacy of God in our lives. He may be number two, number five, or number ten, but he is not number one. We don't realize this, of course, or we would deal with it. We wonder why we are not completely at peace, but we look everywhere else for the root cause, often blaming the people with whom we live and work. We may even begin to blame or doubt God because he seems to have pulled away. But if we look down our list of priorities, we will still find him there, in the lower spot in which we have put him. He is still just as interested in us, but we are not as interested in him.

Many good people live for years with God high on their list of priorities, maybe even in the top ten. They do not think of God every day or pray every day, but they fulfill their worship obligations and try to live according to a moral code. But there are other things, maybe very significant things like work and relationships, that take precedence. God is in the background, not disrespected or disregarded, but not the primary concern. As our priorities slip further, maybe even family and primary relationships get squeezed out of the top ten by some personal project or gain.

In the midst of this drift, God periodically sends a wake-up call to cause us to reconsider our priorities. Often, especially in midlife, a gnawing malaise will drive a personal search that may result in a real conversion. God may have been in our top ten for years but never has been the most important reality that we wake up for in the morning. Through the gift of grace, we can seek help in giving God his rightful place in our lives. The very simple and ordinary way to start this process is to spend a few minutes with God every day, as we would do with people with whom we want to be close. God has been there all the time, waiting somewhere down our list.

The good news is that we don't have to wait until late in life or until we have drifted far away from God or until some disaster has revealed our emptiness, to move God right to the top of the list in our lives. We can do it tomorrow, and the next day, and every day, and our lives will begin to be coherent, and we will be blessed with the peace that is promised to those who truly seek God, the peace we feared we had lost and could not retrieve. God does not like to be left out of our lives, but he does not push, nor does he hold grudges. He is ready and waiting for us when we are ready for him.

2. The Poetry of the Psalms

The psalms are among the oldest poems in the world, having proved their staying power for some three thousand years. A poem includes an experience beyond the content of its words, and that is certainly true of the psalms. Not all the psalms are poetic in the same way or to the same extent. The wisdom psalms, for example, are occasionally dry with moral admonition, while the historical psalms tend to be narrative, but even these psalms have poetic elements. As with any poem, their success depends on capturing an experience of truth in a way that it stirs the reader beyond the obvious content of the words.

Our prayerful use of the psalms may be helped by being alert to two particular poetic elements: imagery, a characteristic of almost all poetry, and parallelism, a special feature of Hebrew poetry. Imagery in good poetry has the ability, by a striking use of the familiar, to produce awareness of the beyond or an understanding of life's deeper meaning. While we can describe God in prosaic terms as almighty, all-knowing, or infinite protector of us and for us, how much more compelling is it to say with the psalmist, "The Lord is my shepherd"? Similarly, longing for God can be described in theological terms as "desire for transcendence." In the psalms this feeling has flesh and blood: it is a thirsty deer, an owl among the ruins, a lonely sparrow on a housetop. It is like eating ashes or drinking tears, or like a parched land desperate for water.

When troubles haunt us, we can sense the authenticity of the psalmist's experience of the same feeling when he says he feels like a sagging wall, a broken-down fence, a worn-out tool, a worm, or a bird that must flee to the mountains. With the help of the psalms, we not only identify our own feelings, but we bring them to prayer.

Parallelism in Hebrew poetry can come through in other languages. One line echoes another in a rhythm of regular beats either to repeat with different words or add to an idea. Consider, for example, the following three passages: "The mouth of the righteous utters wisdom; / his tongue speaks what is right" (Psalm 37:30); "And now, kings, give heed; / take warning, judges on earth" (2:10); and "Even if my father and mother forsake me, / the LORD will take me in" (27:10).

Or a point may be made by contrasting lines: "The LORD watches over all who love him, / but all the wicked he destroys" (Psalm 145:20).

At other times, a progression of thought may spread to three lines: "One conceives iniquity; / is pregnant with mischief, / and gives birth to deception" (Psalm 7:15).

The psalms as poetry invite us, not just to a progression of ideas, but to an experience: being carried on the waves of rolling parallels as the drama of life unfolds from image to image and thought to thought.

Attention to the poetic nature of the psalms can add a dimension to our prayer. Opening our eyes to the array of metaphors and similes, they usher us into the prayer experience of people like ourselves from centuries ago. ⌒◯⌒

3. FLEEING FORGETFULNESS

The longest chapter in St. Benedict's *Rule* is chapter 7 on humility, a virtue he considered fundamental to the Christian monastic life. He used the image of twelve steps of a ladder in describing the various aspects of humility. The first step of humility is "to set the fear of God always before his eyes, and utterly avoid all forgetfulness" (*RB* 7:10).

We may find this a strange way of speaking. What forgetfulness are we to avoid? St. Benedict draws on a familiar theme of the Old Testament: "Be careful not to forget the LORD, your God, by failing to keep his commandments and ordinances and statutes which I enjoin on you today" (Deuteronomy 8:11). What would make someone forget the good God who has brought his people out of slavery into a place of freedom? "Lest, when you have eaten and are satisfied, and have built fine houses and lived in them, and your herds and flocks have increased . . . you then become haughty of heart and forget the LORD, your God" (8:12-14).

In Scripture, encouragement is given for mindfulness, in the instruction to give time off to slaves on the Sabbath: Be mindful of what God has done for you, because "you too were once slaves in the land of Egypt, and the LORD, your God, brought you out from there with a strong hand and outstretched arm" (Deuteronomy 5:15).

According to St. Benedict, mindfulness of God is the basis of the spiritual structure. The Latin word *oblivionem* is translated "forgetfulness." We all know the danger of "spiritual oblivion" and how easy it is to slip into it, especially when things are going well. We forget that God is holding everything together and that we are helpless without him. Sometimes he "opens [our] ears through oppression" (Job 36:15). Psalm 106 portrays the history of Israel as a series of waves of remembering followed by waves of forgetting.

Why is fleeing forgetfulness fundamental to humility? Because it is essential to the fear of God, which puts me in the proper relationship to God, bringing me to realize that God—no one else—is my master, all the time. Whenever I am forgetful of God, I put someone or something else ahead of him, at least momentarily, and whoever or whatever that is becomes my God and for that period receives my obedience (I fear this person or thing, instead of God).

St. Benedict exhorts us to remember that "the divine presence is everywhere and that in every place the eyes of the Lord are watching the good and the wicked" (*RB* 19:1). Early in *The Rule*, he quotes the wonderful promise of God: "My eyes will be upon you and my ears will listen for your prayers; and even before you ask me, I will say to you: Here I am" (Isaiah 58:9, quoted in Prologue, verse 18). The monks' day is punctuated by gatherings for the Divine Office, where "beyond the least doubt we should believe" (*RB* 19:2) that God is present.

What St. Benedict is combating here is what is often described today as practical atheism—professing faith in God but living as if God doesn't exist or as if God's existence is irrelevant. Do I live any differently because of my faith? Are my choices during the day and the way I treat and respond to people affected by my consciousness of the presence of God? If I were brought into court on the accusation of being a Christian, would there be enough evidence to convict me?

St. Paul has another way of talking about fleeing forgetfulness when he says, "Pray without ceasing" (1 Thessalonians 5:17). This statement has worried people who see this as an admonition to be constantly in church or reciting prayers under their breath as they do their work. St. Augustine says it simply means to live with a constant desire for God and heavenly life. Times devoted to prayer are moments when that desire comes to consciousness, so prayer can be there all the time.

Another way to understand praying without ceasing is to compare it to the experience of falling in love or meeting someone we want to know better. Our daily labor becomes a kind of distraction from the person dominating our imagination.

At the Last Supper, Jesus gave us a way to flee forgetfulness of the gift of salvation. The celebration of the Eucharist is the center and pivot of our worship and of our mindfulness. It is a memorial, but in the rich Hebrew sense of making present again. Everything we do can be an echo and fulfillment of Jesus' words "Do this in remembrance of me" (1 Corinthians 11:24).

4. GOD HAS A GOOD MEMORY

Learning in a classroom can sometimes yield more benefits than studying alone. The wrong answer you were preparing to give is corrected when another student volunteers the answer first. Or another student asks a question you hadn't thought of or were reluctant to ask, opening a line of reasoning that might have remained hidden to you.

Those of us with questions about prayer should be grateful to Proba, a Christian widow in North Africa in the early fifth century. In AD 412, Proba wrote a letter to her friend, St. Augustine, asking about prayer, in particular what we should ask for when we pray. In response, Augustine wrote a letter to Proba, expanding on Jesus' words "Your Father knows what you need before you ask him" (Matthew 6:8). He replied to Proba that the Lord God does not need us to tell him what we want "but wants us rather to exercise our desire through our prayers, so that we may be able to receive what he is preparing to give us."[1] The point of prayer is always the person praying, not the many words and thoughts and intentions. These are important in their own way as reinforcing our dependence upon God and our desire for union.

What sometimes can cause frustrations and anxieties when we try to pray is that we might unconsciously think God has a bad memory. We imagine God is sitting with pencil and paper waiting to take down what we say so that he won't forget it. Thus, we feel we must keep reminding God over and over of what we said earlier, and our prayer becomes exhausting and tedious.

The truth is that we are the ones who have bad memories! God has a very good memory. He hears our desires and intentions and doesn't need to be reminded of what we have already asked. So why do we need to keep praying? Because he wants to hear from us: "Cast all your worries upon him because he cares for you" (1 Peter 5:7). Jesus encourages persistence in prayer and even says we need to pray without ceasing (Luke 18:1). It is our constant desire for God and trust in his help, says St. Augustine, that is "praying without ceasing."[2] God becomes the polestar of our life, not just a light we turn on or off according to changing need or whim.

Our prayers of petition do not have to be pressured or frantic. When people ask us to pray for them, let us place them and their needs before God and leave them with God. We may remember to pray for these intentions again, perhaps many more times, and that is good, but their needs are with God. By coming before God, even in complete silence, we will be presenting them without having to say anything at all. We can relax. When we come before God, everyone we love and everything we care about come with us. "Relax," says God. "You are doing your part, and I will do mine." ✑

5. If God Were Only Like Us

We tend to believe that the biblical text we have today has been handed down intact from original documents of the earliest times. But the fact is that we have no original biblical document in the sense of a manuscript from a writer. All of our sources for the biblical text are copies of the originals or of other copies. For centuries the copies were all made by hand and depended on the attention and skill of scribes for accuracy. Inaccuracies inevitably crept in because of human error. The accurate text we have today has been established by the comparison of thousands of manuscripts produced in the early centuries.

Sometimes a scribe would be confused by the text he was copying. Perhaps a word was indecipherable or it was a word that looked like another word or the meaning didn't make sense to him. He might have "corrected" the text according to his knowledge or instincts, even adding or subtracting a word. This would be detected later in the comparison of manuscripts. Often this emendation would be a window into the mind of the scribe, such as when an early scribe changed "our joy" to "your joy" in 1 John 1:4. Both readings make sense, but "our joy" is a more radical Christian insight that the scribe presumed was a mistake.

In the Sermon on the Mount, Jesus taught about prayer by saying, "When you pray, go to your inner room, close the door, and pray to your Father in secret. And your Father who sees in secret will repay you" (Matthew 6:6). Some translations in the past added the word "openly": "The Father who sees in secret will reward you openly." This addition originated with a scribe who was copying the text three hundred years after Matthew's Gospel was written. He thought the word "openly" had been left out in this verse (and in verses 4 and 18), failing to perceive that the point is not that we can see God's reward but that he can see our prayer.

As far as I know, no modern translation incorporates the word "openly," because it has been shown by textual study to be a later addition to Matthew's Gospel. But the addition may point to an agenda that was in the scribe's mind and may be in ours as well. When we make a particular petition in our prayer, asking for healing, good weather for a picnic, or safe travel, if what we ask for is granted, we say, "God heard my prayer." We don't say that when the weather was bad for the picnic. But there are no unanswered prayers. God always answers our prayers, though not always visibly in the way we would like. Like the scribe, when we pray for something, we would prefer that God answer "openly," with something we can see.

The words of Jesus are calling us to pray with faith, which means with a radical trust that God always hears and answers our prayers, whether we can see the results or not. The fourth-century scribe wanted to hold God to account the way human beings hold one another to account. But we can't check up on God. If we pray, he will reward us, openly or in secret, in the way he prefers. Often, but not always, we recognize it when God acts "openly" on our behalf, but if we have the faith that Jesus describes, we will know God answers our prayer whether we see the reward or not, whether it looks like what we expected, and whether it comes now or later. ✑

6. The Leash of Love's Longing

In the early 1980s, Dr. Susan Muto, while a specialist in spiritual formation at Duquesne University in Pittsburgh, was asked to write a series of short articles on what she considered the top ten spiritual classics in Western spirituality. Her first title was familiar, *Abandonment to Divine Providence* by Jean-Pierre de Caussade (1675-1751), but the second had not been as well-known in our time: *The Cloud of Unknowing* by an anonymous English author of the late fourteenth century. *The Cloud of Unknowing* is a classic on contemplative prayer, but it had gone out of common usage until the resurgence of interest in different kinds of prayer animated by Vatican Council II. Now it has become known and loved again, thanks largely to the 1973 edition by Fr. William Johnston, SJ.

The author is simple in his approach and in sharing what he has learned personally in the search for God through prayer. He does not present contemplative prayer in terms of ecstasies that sweep us away, but he refers to the time we set aside for prayer as "the time of the work." We cannot know God in his essence, he says, because between us and God is a "cloud of unknowing," but we can pierce this cloud with darts of love, embracing God not with our intellect, but with our desire. "No one can fully comprehend the uncreated God with his knowledge, but each one, in a different way, can grasp him fully through love" (*The Cloud of Unknowing*, chapter 4).

Being called and drawn into the search for God is described as being pulled by "the leash of love's longing" (chapter 1). Love's longing works both ways, but here it is the longing of God for communion with us. We could not even desire God without his grace: "With exquisite kindness, he awakened desire within you, and binding it fast with the leash of love's longing, drew you closer to himself" (chapter 1).

We may feel distant from God and unworthy of his attention, and so we take very hesitant and tentative steps so as not to be presumptuous. But the beautiful truth is that God wants us, that he is intent on drawing us into his love. Our desire for God is secondary to his desire for us. There is nothing easier than growing in this loving relationship with God, because God is willing to do all the work—all that is, except opening our hearts to him, which is our part. "Mark this. God is a jealous lover. He is at work in your spirit and will tolerate no meddlers. The only other one he needs is you. And all he asks of you is that you fix your love on him and let him alone" (chapter 2). Later in his book, the author alters his leash image: "I want to help you tie the spiritual knot of burning love that will bind you to God in a communion of being and desire" (chapter 47).

The test of our faith and our love is the "cloud of unknowing" that hides God from us. God is present but will not overwhelm us with his presence. "You will feel frustrated, for your mind will be unable to grasp him, and your heart will not relish the delight of his love" (chapter 5). What are we to do? We are to "pierce the cloud" with short prayers of desire that come from the depth of our being. "If you strive to fix your love on him…, I am confident that God in his goodness will bring you to a deep experience of himself" (chapter 3). But the author is also realistic. Our prayer involves toil; it is a work. The labor, he says, is in the "unrelenting struggle" with distractions (chapter 26). We must not give up resisting distractions, for God is waiting for us in the cloud of unknowing.

God is inviting us and drawing us to himself with the leash of love's longing very personally, but he is not drawing us to come to him alone. We are members of a body, "individually parts of one another" (Romans 12:5). Conscious of this, we try to bring many people and many causes into our prayer. This may make our prayer very wordy and busy because we do not want to neglect anyone. The author tells us that it is not necessary to fret about this. Prayer is not mainly asking for this or that but being one with God. In being one with God, I am interceding in the best way. "I tell you this, one loving blind desire for God alone is more valuable in itself, more pleasing to God and to the saints, more beneficial to your own growth, and more helpful to your friends, both living and dead, than anything else you could do" (chapter 9).

Still, sometimes we cannot help but be worried about our prayer. The author of *The Cloud* says not to worry: that the God who is drawing us with the leash of love's longing wants us more than we want him and is just watching for the first sign of our desire for him, only that we turn our head his way, and he will do the rest. "I pray that Almighty God in his great goodness and kindness will teach you himself" how to pray (chapter 34). ⌗

7 . Swatting Gnats

In Arkansas and other warm climates, there is no summertime nuisance more aggravating than being pestered by gnats. There are some species, like buffalo gnats, that can do a lot of harm, but the ordinary, or everyday, variety rarely does physical damage; the gnats just drive you crazy. When you're stopping peacefully to enjoy a sunrise or sunset, taking a walk by a lake, or relaxing in your lawn chair, the gnats won't let you be. You could put up with gnats if they swarmed around your arms or legs, but they prefer eyes and ears, and you simply can't concentrate on your business and ignore them. They demand attention. Unless you have access to a super insect spray, the only thing you can do about gnats is keep swatting them away. But don't think you are going to deter them. They will keep coming back. Even if you could manage to kill a few million of them, there would always be more.

I spend a lot of my day swatting gnats, even when I'm inside—but not the physical kind. There are spiritual gnats that drive me crazy, and swatting them away is a major part of my spiritual work. There are distractions even when I decide to pray. I may do everything right: set aside a time, re-collect myself to break from what I've been doing, and find a quiet place where I won't be interrupted, maybe even before the Blessed Sacrament. I take a deep breath, call on the Lord's help, and here they come. Is that candle crooked? I wonder whether it will rain. Did I lock my car? How far is the sun from the earth? Gnats keep coming, and I keep swatting.

For a long time, I didn't understand about the gnats in my prayer. I took them seriously. I figured the distractions were ruining my prayer and that if I couldn't make them stop coming, I wasn't praying. Now, I know that prayer is in the commitment and the decision to pray, and my decision to pray can remain untouched by the gnats. I just have to keep swatting them with my eyes fixed on Jesus. If I try to mash them one by one, they will win because they will take my attention off Jesus, but if I just keep swatting them as soon as I see them, my prayer remains unbroken.

The same is true with those other gnats, the random thoughts that whirl in and out of my mind: especially those that make me feel guilty, the impatience and the inner judgments about people I don't even know—like that man who is too old to be driving and, besides, is going too slow or like the child who used chalk on the sidewalk when I'm sure he should have been in school or like the young man who let the door close in my face. It's even worse with people I know, because the same judgments about them pop into my mind every day. The mistake here is the same as with distractions. These thoughts are mine only if I own them. My brain is sparking off random thoughts and judgments all the time—it's called being alive—but I don't have to be responsible for them. I can just keep swatting and go peacefully on.

Just as there are summer evenings when I can go out and enjoy a peaceful sunset with no gnats around, there are days when it's much easier to control my thoughts and focus my prayer. I am grateful for those times, and I make the most of them, but I have to be careful about thinking that my prayer or my inner life is better on those days than when I am battered by the gnats. I may actually be doing better on the days gnats are swarming, because I have to struggle to stay true to my decisions and convictions. As T. S. Eliot said, "For us, there is only the trying. The rest is not our business."[3]

I am not defending gnats, and I am not defending distractions and uncharitable thoughts. But I am not going to take any of them too seriously. If they keep coming, I will keep swatting.

8 . The Great Vending Machine

In a famous passage in Georges Bernanos' novel *The Diary of a Country Priest*, the struggling pastor is haunted by recent conversations about prayer. "How can those . . . who pray little or not at all, dare to speak so frivolously of prayer? . . . Have you ever heard of a man of prayer who said that prayer doesn't work?" (103). The idea of prayer "working" has an odd sound, even though we all know what it means. Prayer works when we get what we ask for, and otherwise it doesn't. The priest says that a "man of prayer" doesn't think that way. There is a difference between making occasional prayer petitions and having a prayer life.

The country priest is not thinking of prayer as a series of requests with answers that may or may not go our way, but as a life of communion with God. This constant attitude of prayer will certainly be punctuated by petitions for the many needs that come constantly into view. There is no true communion with God without a loving concern for the needs of others and a sharing of our own desires. But there has to be a bond of relationship when we make our requests; otherwise, our prayers are like a series of unrelated visits to the Office of Appropriations.

The prayer that is a constant desire for God always works, because God desires communion with us even more than we desire communion with him. God is always saying yes to that request. As we grow in communion, as in any relationship, our trust grows, and we know that whatever comes our way is always within the context of God's love for us. We ask for many things for others, but not so much for ourselves, because we believe that God wants to give us what is best for us and knows better than we do what that is. An old man in Ireland was asked why he was always smiling and was so happy. "The Father is very fond of me," was his beautiful response. A proverb says, "God gives the best gifts to those who leave the choice to him."

The same point about prayer might be made in terms of a fable: A man approached the teacher and complained, "I don't see what good it does to pray. I never get what I ask for."

The teacher responded, "Do you ever buy things from a vending machine?"

"Sometimes."

"Do you always get what you want?"

"Yes, if I punch the right buttons and put in the money."

"Does the machine always have what you want?"

"Not always."

"So you don't get anything?"

"No, usually I take something else."

The teacher went on: "When you speak of prayer, it sounds to me as if you are thinking of God as the Great Vending Machine in the Sky."

"What do you mean?" the man responded.

"For you, praying is like punching the buttons and putting the money in. You expect the results you bought. There is a difference though."

"What is that?"

"You don't know what the machine is offering. You tell the Machine in the Sky what it should have for you, and if it doesn't, you kick the machine. You don't take something this machine has if it is different from what you wanted at first. But here is also a similarity between the way you treat a vending machine and the way you treat God."

"And what is that?"

"A vending machine isn't really part of your life. You may not even see one for days, and you don't think of one in the meantime. It's only when you see a machine that you remember you want something." The teacher continued, "That's the way you're treating God. God isn't really a part of your life, someone you live with. You think of God when you go to church, and then the first thought is not about God but about what you want. Unlike a vending machine, God knows all about you and has a personal interest in you. He already knows what you want, but better than that, he knows what is best for you. Did you ever think of asking him simply to give you what is best for you?"

"Not exactly."

"Well, if you ask for that, watch out."

"Why?"

"You might get it."

9. Too Many Things to Pray for

Have you at times felt helpless in trying to keep up with all the intentions and concerns you want to bring to God in prayer? The list grows longer every day. Am I free to remove some intentions from time to time? If I promise to remember somebody in prayer, does that mean only one time, or am I committed to mentioning them in prayer for days and weeks?

The issue may become even more daunting for people who have been introduced to a form of contemplation, such as Centering Prayer or Christian meditation. These methods minimize thoughts and words and, ideally, focus attention on God without words. Since Vatican II there has been a resurgence of this kind of prayer, and it has proved to be transformative to many. But what about prayer intentions? Should someone who devotes time to Centering Prayer every day also set aside a prayer time to bring before God the many needs near and far: health issues of family and friends, needs of the parish and diocese, vocations, cancer research, end to abortion, immigration, terrorism, refugees, the environment, and on and on?

The monastic tradition has something very encouraging and comforting to say on this matter. It is no surprise since monasticism has always had a strong tradition of contemplative prayer and, at the same time, a commitment to prayer for local and worldwide needs as a distinctive part of its vocation.

Attention to this message came some years ago in a surprising way by a commentary on events in South Africa while it was still in the throes of the cruel persecution and discrimination of apartheid. Soon after he received the 1984 Nobel Peace Prize for his fearless stance against apartheid, Archbishop Desmond Tutu of Cape Town spoke in the National Cathedral in Washington. He took the occasion to thank people on behalf of South Africa for their prayers. Interestingly, he did not thank them for their prayers on behalf of South Africa.

Archbishop Tutu was making a deeper connection between the personal prayer of believers throughout the world and the gifts of grace bestowed in South Africa. "A man whose home is going to be demolished tomorrow sets out to pray incredibly, 'God, thank you for loving us.' How can that be except that you have prayed him into the state of grace?" The Archbishop was reaching back to the ancient tradition of the intercessory character of all prayer, communal or personal, vocal or silent, mental or contemplative.

Prayer is a reaching out to God, turning to God. But the Christian tradition understands it, not as a reaching out to a God who is distant, but a descent into the heart where God is waiting. Even in the most private and interior moment, the world and its needs are not far away. The God I meet in this sacred moment is present not only to me but to all creation. He sees me, but he sees as well all the people of the world with their particular situations and needs. When I come before God in my inner sanctuary, I become present, through God, to the whole world and its needs.

God does not need me to tell him of those needs. It is good to mention them, as St. Augustine says, but the benefit of mentioning them is for us. What God needs is my love to be a channel for his grace. He "needs" my help because of his own design to save the world by the Incarnation. When I lay myself open to God in faith and love, I become an instrument of his grace near and far. According to the fourteenth-century classic *The Cloud of Unknowing*, my prayerful love reaches even beyond this world: "I tell you this, one blind loving desire for God alone is more valuable in itself, more pleasing to God and to the saints, more beneficial to your own growth, and more helpful to your friends, both living and dead, than anything else you could do" (chapter 9).

This very consoling doctrine relieves the pressure about keeping track of all our prayer petitions. It is good to have intentions and to make petitions, but we don't need to be frantic if we cannot keep up with all the things we want to pray for. Even prayer without any words is responding to the distress of those in need. "We do not know how to pray as we ought," admits St. Paul, "but the Spirit itself intercedes with inexpressible groanings. And the one who searches hearts knows what is the intention of the Spirit, because it intercedes for the holy ones according to God's will" (Romans 8:26-27). Our descent into our own heart in the silence of prayer is at the same time a plunge into the heart of the world, where God is waiting to meet us and take our love to where it is needed most.

10. You Are My Schedule

Cultures have ways of developing rituals that allow us to make connections with others or to bridge gaps without needing to create a new access each time. We can break the ice of meeting someone new by shaking hands and saying "Good morning" or "How do you do?" The transaction is pre-packaged. We might smooth over an awkward silence on the elevator by talking about the weather or put a visitor at ease by mentioning a common interest or acquaintance. These rituals are picked up from the culture without having to be taught or practiced.

The frantic pace of contemporary society has raised the references to our "busy schedule" to a ritual level. Today a customary ritual for asking a favor or thanking for one is to refer to the other's busy schedule: "Thanks for taking time from your busy schedule" or "I feel badly even asking you this favor because I know how busy you are." On one level we are pressured and oppressed by the multitude of responsibilities crammed into our day; however, we may also be proud of how busy we are. What was once "spreading yourself too thin" is now "multi-tasking." Even if we're not busy, we want to appear busy; otherwise, people might think we are lazy.

When my mother started an ordinary day, she didn't know everything she would have to do before it was over, but she knew it would be busy. She was typical of mothers with small children and of many other people in all walks of life. What is on your schedule is one thing, and what will turn up by the end of the day is another. One thing my mother could count on: several times during the day, often right when she was in the middle of something, one of us children was going to interrupt her with a question, a tattle, a cut, a bruise, or something more creative. We never considered saying, "Thanks for taking time from your busy schedule." We knew, and Mother knew, that we were her schedule.

The trouble with the "busy schedule" ritual is the social atmosphere it can create. Our interactions with one another are sometimes cooperation and at other times interruptions, but this ritual implies that every unexpected encounter is an interruption. With this attitude we may grow more and more protective of our time and become reluctant to share it with anyone.

But the truth is, our time is not really ours. It is God's time of which he gives each of us a share to manage. The best use of God's time is to use it the way God does, by loving. Jesus gave us a hint of how we are to think about the others who come unexpectedly into our day when he said, "I was . . . a stranger and you welcomed me" (Matthew 25:35). Someone asking for your time is not an interruption or a threat, but Christ. St. Benedict picked up on this in telling monks to receive all guests as Christ—not just some, but all—and not just strangers at the door, but even the people with whom we live, who come anew into our lives as guests every day.

Abba John was a respected monk in the ancient Egyptian desert, and people were constantly calling on him. One day an old man asked him for advice but then forgot John's answer before he got home. Later on he told Abba John, "I did not want to overburden you, so I did not come back." Abba John said to him, "Light a lamp and bring some more lamps, and light them from the first." When there was a roomful of lamps, Abba John asked, "Has the first lamp suffered because so many lamps were lit from it?" "No," said the old man. "So it is with John," said the Abba. "Even if everyone in the desert came to me, they would not separate me from the love of Christ."

There are obvious limits on our time and energy. We can't serve everybody all the time, and depending on our circumstances, some people have more right to our attention than others. This is the way it is with a married couple toward each other and their children. But beyond the realm of immediate responsibility, people with needs and requests on our time and energy are constantly moving through our lives. We have to be careful of deciding ahead of time who deserves our attention, of a kind of automatic pilot that tells us we are too busy. Remember, the stranger is Christ, and I cannot judge ahead of time what my proper response should be. Maybe this need is not mine to attend to, but it could be that God wants me to take care of it for him. Cain tried to dodge the issue by asking, "Am I my brother's keeper?" (Genesis 4:9). Even when someone says, "I'm sorry to interrupt your busy schedule," my reflex thought should be, "Not so fast. You are my schedule."

11. To Listen like a Disciple

In the third of the four Servant Songs in the Book of Isaiah, the servant tells of his wake-up call from God which could have a beautiful application for all of us: "Morning after morning / he wakens my ear to hear as disciples do" (Isaiah 50:4). If we wake up to this kind of call, our day begins expectantly, as we wait to hear what God will tell us through our prayer and through the people and events of the day.

What does it mean to listen "as disciples do" or "like one being taught," as another translation has it? To listen like a disciple is different from listening like a teacher. When you listen like a teacher, you are expecting people to tell you what you already know and often what you have taught them. They are graded on how well they are able to tell you what you already know. The best teachers, of course, are able to listen both ways: to know when to listen as a teacher and when to listen as a disciple, able to receive new information or new insights from their students and able to make room for the new information, even when it may run counter to what they had already settled on.

It isn't easy to hear something new, especially the more comfortable we become with what we already know and with our own long-term plans. Listening like a disciple is what makes it possible for anyone to hear a vocation from God. The story of our salvation is, in a way, a series of vocation stories: Abraham, Moses, Amos, Jeremiah, Mary, the apostles. They were listening like disciples when the call came. But how many others might God have called before Abraham said yes? Maybe they weren't open to something new, especially something that would change their lives. We know about the ones who were ready for God to break into their lives.

But not always totally ready. Moses initially said, "Here I am" (Exodus 3:4), but when he began to understand the scope of what God was calling him to, he had second thoughts. "Who am I that I should go to Pharaoh and bring the Israelites out of Egypt?" (3:11). He began backpedaling and tried several ways to get the Lord to change his mind. Eventually, Moses accepted the call and allowed God to change the whole future direction of his life. When Moses woke up that morning, he had no idea that this day would be different, but by the end of that day, all his future days were changed; he had become God's prophet to save God's people because he had been able to listen like a disciple.

Mary was completely ready when her call came. She asked for more information to be sure she understood and then said, "I am the handmaid of the Lord. May it be done to me according to your word" (Luke 1:38). Paul was perplexed by the voice from heaven and then stunned to hear it was the voice of Jesus. He had to reorganize his whole worldview and open himself to possibilities that would have been absurd in his earlier system of thinking. But he was not too proud to hear a completely new word, to let his life take a completely new direction.

Obviously, listening like a disciple comes to bear in discerning a vocation in the Church. The call to be a religious or priest may come at any time, but it usually happens in the early years when our ears are still more easily open to new possibilities.

These examples are exceptional calls and one-time events. But our life of discipleship is ongoing, an everyday walk. Parents and teachers may never abdicate their responsibility of guiding and teaching those under their charge. But at the same time, they need to beware of getting to a point where they stop in their tracks. There is always something more to learn. For all of us, it may be hardest to listen with new awareness to people with whom we live and work and hear every day and to those whom we have pigeonholed by some prejudice. Can anything good come out of Nazareth?

Listening as a disciple requires silence, inner silence. We cannot really hear if our minds are busy grading other people's information or already formulating a response. A few years ago, a biology instructor in England took his class on a spring field trip into the woods to experience the sights and sounds of the forest. At one point he told them to be absolutely silent so that they could hear the smaller sounds, like the rustling of leaves in the breeze and the scurrying of small animals. In the silence they began to hear a different sound, a faint human voice. They hurried to the source, an abandoned cistern, into which a man had fallen several days before. They would not have heard him and could not have saved him if they had not been listening. ∽

PART II

PRAYER IN
SUFFERING

12 . A Nursing Home Retreat

O ccasionally, when I return to the Abbey after visiting the sick or shut-ins, I will remark to one of the monks that I have been on a nursing home retreat. What I mean by this is that, whether in a nursing home, a hospital, or a private home, on that occasion I have had the grace of visiting someone whose acceptance of a desperate condition is so filled with faith and peace that it affected me like the spiritual power of a retreat. Perhaps few words were exchanged and sometimes none at all, but the word of God has been proclaimed by the presence of holiness.

In *The Old Man and the Sea*, Ernest Hemingway introduces the fisherman Santiago with this description: "Everything about him was old except his eyes and they were the same color as the sea and were cheerful and undefeated" (10). On my nursing home retreats, I have met many people with these kind of eyes.

As in any good retreat, the experience is not just inspiring but unsettling, making me look at myself. How will I be when I reach that stage in my life? Unless death intervenes while I am still up and around, I will be going there. We all will. We will have to deal with diminishment and dependence. How will I do that? Will I be a trial to those who care for me and visit me, or will I be a gift, as so many are to me?

Everyone must undergo suffering along the road of life. Some of it is our own fault, the result of our decisions and actions. If we can deal properly with suffering at all, it is this kind that we can handle. The test is in dealing with undeserved suffering, especially the kind that could have been prevented by others or, above all, the kind purposely inflicted on us by others. Does the suffering we endure become a sharing in the cross, a dying with Jesus, and therefore redemptive, or does it seethe in anger and self-pity? Whatever pattern we have established will go with us to our nursing home bed. In commenting on the parable of the house built on rock or sand, John Cassian says that "when mistreatment inflames the fire of anger in us, it is not because of the abuse received, but because our house was built on sand and gave way at the slightest push" (*Conferences* 18:3).

Pain is an essential part of life. If we never got our fingers burned, we would not know the danger of fire. But what bothers us is the needless pain and the unreasonable suffering. This would have been there whether or not Christ came, but with redemption a whole new opportunity for dealing with suffering entered the world. Scripture tells us that the Savior himself had to walk this road: "Was it not necessary that the Messiah should suffer these things and enter into his glory?" (Luke 24:26). The author of Hebrews makes the amazing statement, "Son though he was, he learned obedience from what he suffered; when he was made perfect, he became the source of eternal salvation for all who obey him" (5:8-9). With Paul, we can understand that our sufferings even play a role in Christ's work of redemption: "Now I rejoice in my sufferings for your sake, and in my flesh I am filling up what is lacking in the afflictions of Christ on behalf of his body, which is the church" (Colossians 1:24).

It would be easier if we could choose our sufferings. We see one saint chiding another in a letter of Francis de Sales to Jane Frances de Chantal: "You're willing to accept the cross as long as it is the one you select."[4] Abbot John Chapman gives us the image of God as a sculptor trying to bring our true self out of the raw block of marble we are. We do not understand the reason for the hammer blows, and we rebel. St. Teresa of Avila says even if we can bear suffering, we want immediate results, and we suspect that nothing is happening, that God is doing nothing in our lives. "That is the kind of people we are," she writes in the *Way of Perfection*. "Ready cash is the only wealth we understand."

When we are young and climbing the hill of life, we are oblivious to the challenges that will come with aging and diminishment. We are not exactly in denial, but those things are not a reality for us; they haven't yet come on the screen. Denial may come later on. But the time to prepare for a graceful and hopeful old age is before we get there. It isn't accidental, the luck of the draw for the chosen. The people who preach Christ to me in the time of their physical diminishment have been suffering with Christ throughout their lives. They may not be able to make a decision to do that now, but they made the decision previously, and it still carries them now.

13. THE POWER OF HELPLESS PRAYER

In October, 1978, ten years after his ordination as a priest in Prague, Fr. Miloslav Vlk was picked up by state authorities and prohibited from exercising any priestly ministry. He was forced to withdraw from association with Church activity and became a window cleaner in downtown Prague. During this time, he was haunted by questions about his vocation and wondered whether he had any priestly identity at all. He could not lead, worship with, console, or instruct his people. He was troubled by discouragement and by doubts about whether in his present status, to all appearances a layman, his priesthood meant anything.

Then he had an illumination in which he realized, as he wrote later, that "Jesus arrived at the climax of his priesthood when, nailed to the cross, he could not walk, perform miracles, nor preach, but—abandoned—suffered in silence" (*A Lenten Pilgrimage—Journeying with Jesus*). Jesus did the most he could for people, achieving salvation and redemption, when he yielded completely to the Father's will, giving up personal control and power completely. This prayer and offering was his ministry. This realization gave Fr. Vlk a new sense of his priestly identity and service, and it also gave him peace as he continued to wash windows until he was able to return to regular ministry in 1989 at the beginning of what would become the Velvet Revolution in Czechoslovakia.

All of us have times when we feel helpless to do what we think we should. It may be on the national or international level, as we watch developments that we know can only lead to suffering and ruin. But this is not where we suffer most often. Mostly it is closer to home, as when parents watch their grown children going down wrong paths or see them suffering in their own families, or when someone we love is sunk in bitterness or is terminally ill. We feel helpless, like Fr. Vlk. What can we do?

This is where the mystery of redemption comes to our rescue. In terms of this world, when we are helpless, we are powerless. However, in the mystery of Christ on the cross, as Fr. Vlk learned, it is altogether different. We can unite ourselves to Christ in his suffering, trusting in the love of the Father and yielding to his will. Fr. Jacques Philippe puts it succinctly in his wonderful little book, *Interior Freedom:* "The more devoid of means our love is, the purer and greater it is" (59). St. Paul experienced this in his ministry and said, "When I am weak, then I am strong" (2 Corinthians 12:10). What better can we do for our loved ones who are struggling than simply lift them up to the Lord while holding them in our hearts and in our prayers? We know what we want for them, but maybe we don't know what is best for them. Our Father knows and can do infinitely more than we can for them.

This is why the highest form of Christian prayer is wordless, simply spending time with God in silence. The early Christians referred to *monologistos* prayer, prayer of a single word or phrase, especially the name of Jesus, or the Jesus Prayer, recited over and over, as a means of focusing. Mother Teresa was asked what she said to God in prayer, and she said, "I just listen." And what does God say to you? "He just listens." Prayer has many forms that we may always incorporate into our practice, but the progression of prayer is from instructing God about what he should do toward offering him our presence in an attitude of humble supplication and submission.

Life brings periods of helplessness when we are confined to bed, very sick or immobilized because of an accident or trauma. It is easy to be overwhelmed by frustration or depression during these times. These are times when, if we understand the power of helpless prayer, the distress may be lessened or healed by hope. This is even more important for people whose helplessness will be permanent because of a major disability or because of the natural onset of the diminishment that comes with age. Our nursing homes contain people undergoing all kinds of suffering, especially that of abandonment. The amazing thing is that in those beds of helplessness, we encounter some people who are radiant with peace and joy. What is their secret? Perhaps their faith has led them to understand the power of helpless prayer.

14. God or the Works of God

S ix days after he was named coadjutor, Archbishop of Saigon (now Ho Chi Minh City), Fr. Francis-Xavier Nguyen Van Thuan was imprisoned by the Communist government of Vietnam. He spent thirteen years, from 1975 to 1988, in a "reeducation camp," including nine of those years in solitary confinement. Archbishop Van Thuan did not despair during his dark time in prison. He was sustained in hope by his prayers and unyielding faith. He smuggled out messages of hope to his people on scraps of paper that were later published in *The Road of Hope*.

In November,1988, Archbishop Van Thuan was transferred to house arrest in Hanoi, 700 miles away from his diocese. Three years later he was allowed to leave Vietnam to go to Rome, with the provision that he would not be able to return. In 1994, Pope John Paul II named him the president of the Pontifical Council for Justice and Peace, and in 2000 asked him to be the preacher for an annual spiritual retreat for himself and the Roman Curia. His conferences have been published under the title *Testimony of Hope*.

Archbishop Van Thuan describes his years of solitary confinement in a cell without windows, in extreme heat and humidity. Lights would be left on for days at a time; then they would be turned off to create complete darkness for days at a time. He was tormented by the abandonment of his diocese and the inability to minister to his desperate people.

A turning point in his life came in an experience in which he heard a voice saying to him, "Why do you torment yourself like this? You must distinguish between God and the works of God. All the many works you want to do for your people are excellent. These are God's works, but *they* are not God. If God wants you to leave all of these works, do it right away, and have faith in him! God can do things infinitely better than you can." He says this message gave him new peace and completely changed his way of thinking. It helped him survive ordeals that were almost beyond his endurance. "To choose God and not the works of God. This is the foundation of the Christian life in every age."

The archbishop began to be more attentive to the possibilities of every moment. He realized that by his fidelity and his prayer, he was still serving his people outside, even in a deeper way. Additionally, he found that a new field of ministry had opened for him: serving his Communist jailors. He had previously overlooked this opportunity. The guards had been instructed not to speak with him, because he was dangerous. With his smiles and kindness, he broke through this wall, and he began to tell them of his experiences and ask about their families. One eventually smuggled in some pieces of wood from which he made a small cross. "They became my friends."

Another of the guards had been assigned to study Latin to read subversive Catholic documents. He asked the archbishop to teach him a Latin song. As a result, the atheistic guard was soon singing "Veni, Creator Spiritus" several times a day in a loud voice. "Little by little I realized that the Holy Spirit was using a Communist policeman to help an imprisoned bishop pray when he was too weak or depressed. I would not have been allowed to sing a Catholic song there myself."[5]

The day after his arrest, the archbishop had been able to write a letter asking friends for some basic needs, in which he included "medicine for my stomachache." A small bottle of wine came back labeled "stomach medicine" and also a flashlight containing small hosts. "Every day, with three drops of wine and a drop of water in the palm of my hand, I would celebrate Mass. This was my altar, and this was my cathedral!"

A year after he preached this retreat Archbishop Van Thuan was named a cardinal by Pope John Paul II. He died in September 2002, at the age of 74. ⌒⌒

PART III

CALLING AND COMMITMENT

15. Community Prayer

Afamiliar description of the life of a Benedictine monk is *ora et labora*, translated "pray and work," and it gives a good picture of the regular and steady rhythm of the daily monastic schedule. Slogans cannot cover everything, however, and shouldn't be viewed as a complete explanation of a complex reality.

Two weaknesses of this formula have long been noted. First, a major ingredient of the spiritual program of St. Benedict has been left out: *lectio divina* (divine reading), to which, according to his *Rule*, two to four hours per day are allotted, depending on the season. So "pray, read, and work" would be a more complete description of the Benedictine life. The second weakness is that whether with two major ingredients or three, the implication is that these are completely separate exercises: praying takes place at certain hours, reading at others, and work at still others. To Benedict, however, life is a seamless garment, and all of it is in some way prayer, the desire and search for God. There is no division into sacred and profane in what he calls "the house of God" (*RB* 31:19). The monk in charge of material goods is cautioned to "regard all utensils and goods of the monastery as sacred vessels of the altar" (31:10). A good key to Benedict's understanding is his description of the Divine Office, or Liturgy of the Hours, when the community comes together for regular times of community prayer. St. Benedict calls this exercise *Opus Dei*, or "The Work of God," and indicates its vital place in the monastic program by saying, "Nothing should be put ahead of the Work of God" (43:3).

A mistaken notion of this phrase is that in our Divine Office, we are working *for* God. We are taking time out of our day, breaking away from our own work and other interests, to devote to God and his purposes. Instead of working for ourselves at those hours, we are working for God. But our community prayer is, rather, the Work *of* God in which we are privileged to participate at those times in a special way. And what is this work: the redemption and salvation of God's children throughout the world. St. Pachomius, an early monastic founder (292–348) is famously quoted as saying, "I became a monk to save the world."

Before St. Benedict, community life itself was sometimes referred to as the "Work of God." Benedict does not deny this interpretation, but he puts the focus of the monk's participation in God's work in the community prayer. Other work may seem to be more practical or productive, but that is an illusion he wants to combat by centering all the monks' striving in their times of prayer together.

Community prayer is an extension of personal prayer. In fact, community prayer is of little worth unless it is undergirded by the daily personal prayer and striving of the individual monks. The main focus even of individual prayer in the monastic community is not on personal spiritual growth in holiness, though that is an inevitable corollary. The emphasis is on participating in God's work in the salvation of the people and bringing them to God.

An insight into the monastic prayer impulse was given by Archbishop Tutu of South Africa in a speech in Washington in the 1980s during the violent imposition of discrimination in the form of apartheid in his country. In the name of South Africa, he thanked those who had been praying. He did not thank them for praying for South Africa nor imply that they had specified South Africa in their prayers. He was dipping into a deeper stream. When I pray, especially in silent attention without words, I descend into my center where God is indwelling. God knows all the needs of the world at every minute. He is glad for me to tell him about them, but his desire is for the complete availability of my heart, which can then be used as a channel for grace anywhere in the world. As God, he would not "need" my help, but by the Incarnation he has involved me in the work he could easily do by himself and is waiting for my participation.

Archbishop Tutu had a strong grasp of the ancient monastic tradition of prayer and understood this. People who prayed had been helping South Africa, whether they had intended to do so or not. This insight was understood and expressed in two simple lines by the Jesuit poet St. Robert Southwell, martyred in Reformation England: "Not where I breathe do I live, / But where I love."[6] Through my prayer, God can take my love anywhere in the world. I will never know in this life to whom I am ministering through prayer. I do not need to know, but I must simply persevere and leave the rest to God.

When a community of monks come from their personal individual communion with God to pray together as one, they are truly doing the Work of God and ministering to the whole world. Where God will use their ministry of prayer on any given day is known only by God, but they can have the peaceful confidence that through their love, grace is touching people who need it somewhere in the world. ⌦

16. Our Daily Bread

In his 2007 book *Jesus of Nazareth: From the Baptism in the Jordan to the Transfiguration,* Pope Benedict XVI devotes several pages to the wording of a prayer we use every day in public worship and private devotion: the Our Father. When we pray, "Give us this day our daily bread," we are glossing over two much-discussed words. While the Lord's Prayer appears in two versions in the New Testament, a longer form in Matthew 6:9-15 (which we follow in daily usage) and a shorter form in Luke 11:2-4, both contain the prayer for "daily bread" and use identical words in Greek: *arton epi-ousion.* As the pope notes, there is a long-standing dispute about what the Greek word *epi-ousion,* which we translate as "daily," actually means. The word doesn't appear anywhere else in Greek literature, only here in the two texts of the Lord's Prayer in Matthew and Luke.

St. Jerome (347–420) gave a silent witness to the problem that was already well-known in his time when he translated the Gospels into Latin: he used the word "daily" for Matthew's version and "supersubstantial" for Luke's, even though he was translating the same Greek word in both cases. Other early translations had other variations: perpetual, necessary, future, bread of tomorrow. In the latter two instances, the idea was "Give us this day the bread for tomorrow," meaning the sustenance we will need to live faithfully as we move into the future. Pope Benedict notes that among the variations, the two principal interpretations are "what is necessary for existence" (daily bread) and "bread for the future." Bread for the future might be for this earthly life or for eternity.

The pope also notes another important dimension. The Fathers of the Church were practically unanimous in understanding this petition of the Lord's Prayer to refer to the Eucharist (see *Catechism of the Catholic Church*, 2837). This does not replace the idea of daily bread in the physical sense but adds the crucial insight that the daily bread that sustains and is necessary for real existence is the Bread of Life, which Jesus describes when he says, "Whoever eats this bread will live forever" (John 6:58).

Another insight was provided by the late Fr. Eugene LaVerdiere, a biblical scholar of the Congregation of the Blessed Sacrament. He concluded that the Greek-speaking Christian community invented the word to describe their unique religious observance, a meal unlike any other. A confirmation of this insight may be in St. Jerome's translation of *epi-ousion* in the Gospel of Luke as "supersubstantial," a word he apparently coined to portray the two parts of the Greek word: *epi*, meaning "above" or "beyond," and *ousia*, meaning "substance" or "reality." It would then have the sense of "above the ordinary," or extraordinary, and be an in-family word for the Eucharist: our "*epi-ouson*-bread."

Fr. LaVerdiere calls attention to the word "our" in both versions of the Lord's Prayer. We are not just asking for daily bread, but *our* daily bread, which for Christians is uniquely the Eucharist. In this sense, the third-century priest St. Cyprian of Carthage commented, "We pray that 'our' bread, Christ, be given to us every day, that we, who remain and live in Christ, may not depart from his healing power and from his body."[7]

As noted earlier, the Eucharistic understanding of "our daily bread" doesn't erase its other dimensions. In the Lord's Prayer, we still pray for our physical sustenance. St. Augustine (354–430) adds a third aspect, the bread of the word of God, and summarizes in these words: "We must take all three meanings conjointly; that is to say, that we are to ask for all at once as daily bread, both the bread necessary for the body, and the visible hallowed bread, and the invisible bread of the word of God."[8]

There is another slight difference in the two traditions of the Lord's Prayer that may enrich the application to our own spiritual journey. Matthew's version has "Give us *today* our daily bread," while Luke, using a different expression, has "Give us *each day* (or "day by day" in the King James version) our daily bread." These variations, reflecting the adaptation of the prayer in its use in early Christian communities, express both the immediacy of today's need and the ongoing need every day. ∽

17. THE WORD OF GOD GROWS

Three times in the Acts of the Apostles, St. Luke summarizes a period of growth of membership in the new Christian community with this curious statement: "The word of God grew" or "The word of the Lord grew" (Acts 6:7; 12:24; 19:20). This has given translators fits, wondering how there could be additions to the revelation. As a result, most English and other modern translations avoid a literal rendering of the Greek words and treat them as a statement about the progress of the preaching of the gospel message: for example, "The word of God continued to spread."

Modern biblical study has thrown helpful light on this problem and confirmed that St. Luke, always recognized as a very careful writer, did not make a slip of the wrist (three times!) in using this phrase but did so purposely to make an important point about the proclamation of the gospel. In fact, his insight is very timely when the New Evangelization is so much a focus of recent papal teaching and Church documents.

St. Luke envisioned from the beginning that he would write a two-part work—the Gospel of Luke and the Acts of the Apostles—about the life of Jesus in the first book and about the beginning of the life of the Church, the community of his followers, in the second. He was an author fond of parallels and pairings and, in a general way, wrote the story of the emerging Church as a parallel to the life of Jesus in the Gospel. For example, before Jesus begins his saving ministry, he is filled with the Holy Spirit at his baptism; and the outpouring of the

Holy Spirit on the disciples at Pentecost marks the beginning of the life and ministry of the Church.

"The word of the Lord grew" passages in Acts recall a text early in Luke's Gospel when after the presentation of Jesus in the temple and the responses of Simeon and Anna, the family returns to Nazareth: "The child grew and became strong, filled with wisdom; and the favor of God was upon him" (Luke 2:40). The Greek word used for "grew" in this text is the same as in the Acts passages about the word of God and is even in the same tense. The child grew, and later the word of the Lord grew. What is Luke implying by this striking usage? The clue is given in the first of the three Acts passages. The statement, "The word of God grew," is followed by this explanation: "the number of the disciples in Jerusalem increased greatly; even a large group of priests were becoming obedient to the faith" (Acts 6:7). The word of God grew in the addition of new members to the community of believers.

Sometimes we are tempted to limit the word of God to something communicated only through the Bible or by the preaching of the gospel. But the word of God is Jesus and the life he shares. Luke wants us to be aware that the word of God is embodied in believers and is communicated through their lives. We recognize here a main theme in the teaching of Pope Francis: "Let us all remember this: one cannot proclaim the Gospel of Jesus Christ without the tangible witness of one's life . . . [Preach] with your life . . ." (Pope Francis, Homily, April 14, 2013).

St. Luke makes the same point in a different way earlier in the Acts of the Apostles when describing the growth of the Christian community. Instead of saying people joined the apostolic society, he says, "Yet more than ever, believers in the Lord, great numbers of men and women, were *added to the Lord*" (Acts 5:14, emphasis added). We are familiar with Paul's imagery of the body of Christ. Luke's way of putting it is that in joining the Christian community, one becomes part of the proclamation, part of the word of God: we are added to the Lord. And so, every time a person accepts salvation in Christ and membership in his Church, the word of God grows.

Whether or not one really becomes part of the proclamation of the gospel depends on one's own response and faithful discipleship. Pope Francis reminded us of this in The Joy of the Gospel in speaking of "fervent evangelization": "It is not the same thing to have known Jesus as not to have known him, not the same thing to walk with him as to walk blindly, not the same thing to hear his word as not to know it, and not the same thing to contemplate him, to worship him, to find our peace in him, as not to" (§ 266). As our faith deepens, our life proclaims Jesus beyond any words, and through the faithful life of the disciples of Jesus, the word of God continues to grow.

18. JUDGE AND JURY

Years ago, I routinely picked up hitchhikers. It was a safer world then, and I never experienced any problems. In fact, often I was the greater beneficiary of our time together. At one point, within a relatively short interval, I gave rides to two men who were facing very similar life challenges. I was struck by the radically different solutions the two were contemplating. Both of them were on the road because of critical conditions at home involving finances, sickness, and other stresses. One man was simply running away, "starting over," leaving his family to fend for themselves. His conversation was in terms of what he wanted and what he needed. The other was heading to another state in response to a potential job opportunity. Unlike the first man, his conversation was not focused on himself; it was all in terms of his family and what they needed. He was not running away; he was running toward something new and unknown that he would have rather not had to face. Despite the difficulty to him personally, he would not leave his family in the lurch. He was a religious man and expressed the deep conviction that "the man upstairs" would take care of him and his family. But he knew it would probably get worse before it got better.

These two men were confronted by crisis in almost identical terms. One isolated himself in his crisis and had come to equate the problem with his family. He hoped to solve the problem by excluding the family from his life. The other saw himself as involved in the crisis along with his family and intended to face it, for better or worse, united with them.

In one of his retreat conferences, Fr. Bernard Basset records a self-written (and self-serving) epitaph from 1830 inscribed on a marble tablet in an old English church: "George Parker, a native and constant resident of this village, by pursuing a path of undeviating rectitude, warmly endeared himself to a select circle of friends, and firmly secured the esteem of all who had the happiness of his acquaintance; while to these he was an able and faithful counselor, to the deserving poor he was a ready patron." George Parker was clearly pleased with himself, though we ourselves may shudder at his pompous language. Two of his phrases—"select circle of friends" and "deserving poor"—betray a snobbish attitude that is not uncommon today. These are control words. Parker set himself up as the judge and jury of who deserved his attention. Thus, he justified a policy of inclusion and exclusion, accepting people or cutting them out. He is a different version, though subtler, of the hitchhiker who wanted to solve his problems by getting rid of his family.

But aren't all of us tempted to control whom we let into our lives and especially to whom we give our attention and care? But belief in a provident God entails the conviction that there is another who sends people into my life, selecting for me those who will be the best support for my weakness and the best challenge to my self-centeredness. This is the way Jacob met Rachel and Laban, and the way Paul met Barnabas and Peter. For parents, it is the way babies are conceived and accepted; and for babies, it is the way they enter a given family. Sometimes we have to let people go from our lives or move away from them when that seems best for all concerned. But we must be careful about selecting and excluding according to our wishes and whims.

Science and technology are giving us more and better tools for controlling what we classify as problems or inconveniences, especially by eliminating them. When this carries over to people, it supports more efficient methods of abortion and better machines to accept or reject the unborn according to gender, health, and even secondary characteristics. We find ways to eliminate or forestall problems, whether they are immigrants, the elderly, or those who are infirm.

Jesus' message might seem naïve in such a world: "I was . . . a stranger and you welcomed me, naked and you clothed me, ill and you cared for me" (Mathew 25:35-36). The kingdom of God is a place of inclusiveness and sharing; its alternative is exclusion and isolation. That darkness may be safe, but it is very lonely. ∽

19. A Rope or a Chain

Several years ago, I attended a meeting of abbots in Corpus Christi, Texas. During a break in the sessions, we were given a tour of the large aircraft carrier in the harbor, the USS Lexington. The ship was anchored to the pier by large ropes. We asked the guide why a ship weighing 42,000 tons was not anchored by chains. He said chains would not be nearly as secure as ropes. A rope is a collection of small fibers wound together. Any single strand could hold only a little, but wound together, many strands make a very strong rope, even if one or several strands should break. But a chain is only as strong as its weakest link.

Similarly, a life is a collection of small acts. A life of integrity is very strong but not built suddenly, and it is not formed by a few large acts, like links in a chain, but by many small acts forming the strands of a rope, lengthening and intertwining in the same direction over years and years. A life that is inconsistent doesn't have a theme and may take a new direction with each influence or temptation. It is like a series of links in a chain instead of a rope made of long interwoven fibers. That kind of life keeps starting over. It is like hopping from stone to stone in crossing a creek instead of using a bridge. The next step may not be obvious, and the series of stones may be hard to follow because they are not in a straight line. You may even find, in a moment of panic, that the stone chain doesn't reach to the other side.

A life without a strong binding theme may break down in front of small temptations: I will give in this time, but just this one time. Just this time I will cheat, lie, backbite, or skimp on my work. Just this once I will not pray, not go to church, not do my part, not be kind, not be true. This is where lives break down, at that weak link: just this time. We start over, but have no long-term direction, and our new act can only form the next link in a chain, not extend a strand in weaving a faithful life. But there is hope: we are not doomed because of a history of weak links, but we may begin at any time with small consistent acts to weave a strong life.

The great lives are woven from thousands of small acts of integrity. No "just this time"—I will do what is right, what is loving, what is true, every time. I will keep my promise, my commitment, every time, whether things go well or ill. It makes no difference whether I am at home or on the road, whether someone sees me or not. I have decided what the purpose of my life is and have chosen to pursue it. The threads of my life will not be broken by things outside me. Eventually, a life of great strength is built by these small but consistent fibers.

In her poem "The House at Rest," Carmelite poet Jessica Powers asks the question "How does one hush one's house, / each proud possessive wall, each sighing rafter?" In answering, she paraphrases a teaching of St. John of the Cross: "Virtue it is that puts a house at rest." A basic concept of virtue is "moral excellence," and in the Christian tradition, a virtue is a habit formed by daily decisions in seeking what is right and good. These daily decisions build the tiny threads that make up the rope of a strong and coherent life. The point of "The House at Rest" is that, in addition to the strength that comes from virtuous living, there is the unexpected benefit of inner peace.

With peace comes patience and trust in God, and the "fruit of the Spirit" (Galatians 5:22): "love, joy . . . faithfulness, gentleness," and all its other gifts (5:22-23).

Something more comes from this kind of life: it becomes a gift to others. A virtuous and faithful life becomes a rope to which others can cling, a point of reference, and a source of hope for other lives. The communion of saints is a lifeline. "And thus," says Blessed John Henry Newman, whose own life seemed winding and confused but was a resolute and unyielding search for the truth, "in a dark world Truth still makes way in spite of the darkness, passing from hand to hand" (*Parochial and Plain Sermons* 293). ∽

PART IV

THE CHARACTER OF GOD

20. THE QUALITY OF MERCY

An unfortunate translation in the story in Luke's Gospel often entitled "The Penitent Woman" gave rise to a misconception that forgiveness of sins depends on one's fervor. The sentence that caused the trouble was Luke 7:47, which came to generations of English-speaking Christians in the Catholic Douay-Rheims translation of the Bible and in the Protestant King James Version, with slight differences in wording, as having Jesus say, "Many sins are forgiven her because she has loved much."

This isn't what Jesus said, though that translation of the Greek is literally defensible. What he meant and what he said are clarified by the context, especially by the parable he told. He didn't say that her love earned the forgiveness that he was now going to give her, but that her love showed that she had already been forgiven. It was the opposite of what it seemed. She wasn't forgiven because she loved; she loved because she was forgiven.

The scene is set in the house of Simon, who has invited Jesus to dine with him. In the course of the meal, a "sinful woman in the city" enters and proceeds to wash Jesus' feet with her tears, kissing them and anointing them with precious oil. Simon is offended by the woman but even more by Jesus, who lets her touch him.

Jesus knows what is going through Simon's mind and tells a parable to offer him illumination.

"Two people were in debt to a certain creditor; one owed five hundred days' wages, and the other owed fifty. Since they were unable to repay the debt, he forgave it for both. Which of them will love him more?" Simon said in reply, "The one, I suppose, whose larger debt was forgiven." (Luke 7:41-43)

Jesus confirms Simon's answer and goes on to show that Simon's love and consideration for him is much less than that if the woman. Simon has not done any of the customary rituals of welcome, which was his duty, but the woman has done so extravagantly, even though it wasn't her duty. The Jerusalem Bible catches beautifully the point of the parable and Jesus' interpretation of what is going on in the woman's life: "I tell you that her sins, her many sins, must have been forgiven her, or she would not have shown such great love." And without naming Simon, Jesus interprets his reaction to the woman and to himself: "It is the man who is forgiven little who shows little love" (Luke 7:47, JB).

The teaching of Jesus in this story has important consequences for us. It is not any action of ours, even our love, that brings us forgiveness, but the love of God for us. We do not have to earn God's forgiveness in any way, but simply open our hearts to it. God's forgiveness is immediate when we turn to him. And when that happens, our lives begin to change from the inside. Freed from sin, we are able to love, and to spread love to others.

Although we have received forgiveness and have felt the weight lifted, we need someone to confirm that for us, as Jesus did for the woman: "Your sins are forgiven" (Luke 7:48). In this case, Jesus is not saying, "I forgive your sins" but, rather, "I confirm the forgiveness you have already received, which is evident in the love you are showing." The Sacrament of Reconciliation continues this ministry of Jesus in the Church. When the priest says the words of absolution, it may be that our sins are being forgiven at that moment or—and this is probably often the case—our sins were forgiven earlier when we turned back to God and decided to ask for forgiveness. In this case, the priest is confirming in the name of the Church what has happened: "Your sins are forgiven."

The point we must take away from this story is that Jesus is always accessible and always ready to forgive. We do not have to rely on a good record in the past nor holy feelings in the present to get his attention and to receive forgiveness. He is always eager to forgive immediately and free us from the burden that has weighed us down, so that we may respond in gratitude and begin to live in love.

21. CONTEMPLATION AS THE NEW EVANGELIZATION

In the fall of 2012, Pope Benedict XVI convoked a synod on the New Evangelization. Roughly 300 bishops, leaders of religious orders, and other invited participants met in Rome October 7–28. In a surprising move, to stress that the challenge of a new Christian evangelization is not limited to the Catholic Church, Pope Benedict invited Archbishop Rowan Williams, Primate of the Anglican Church, to give a keynote address early in the synod. The archbishop's address, drawing often on Catholic sources, was like a laser beam cutting through the clutter of terminology to the foundation of evangelization in the contemplative gaze of God.

Archbishop Williams began by recalling the perspective of the early Church, that the Christian gospel is not adding a layer of information unrelated to the aspirations of humanity, but it is proclaiming that in Christ it is at last possible to be fully human. "To be fully human is to be recreated in the image of Christ's humanity" (Address to the Synod of Bishops, October 11, 2012). The way to be thus re-created is not mainly by reflecting on and absorbing ideas about God, but by turning our inner gaze to God: to contemplate the God who reveals himself in Christ. The first step in evangelization is being receptive, opening ourselves to the fullness our heavenly Father wishes to pour into our hearts. This is the pattern Jesus used with the first evangelizers, the Twelve, calling them first "to be with him" before sending them out to preach and heal (Mark 3:14). We are reduced to silence in the divine presence and must first be purified ourselves of false fantasies about God. We must know God personally. In this way we become ready to offer our gift to the world.

> The face we need to show to our world is the face of a humanity in endless growth towards love, a humanity so delighted and engaged by the glory of what we look towards that we are prepared to embark on a journey without end to find our way more deeply into it, into the heart of the Trinitarian life. (Address to the Synod of Bishops, October 11, 2012)

Archbishop Williams is here paraphrasing the insight of St. Paul, that only by "gazing with unveiled face on the glory of the Lord" (2 Corinthians 3:18) will Christians be able to break through the veil of indifference and unbelief that covers the world. "God who said, 'Let light shine out of darkness,' has shone in our hearts to bring to light the knowledge of the glory of God on the face of [Jesus] Christ" (4:6).

We don't gaze on God to become self-absorbed—just the opposite. In his message for Lent, 2013, shortly before his resignation, Pope Benedict XVI said, "The Christian life consists in continuously scaling the mountain to meet God and then coming back down . . . so as to serve our brothers and sisters with God's own love" (section 3). In Pope Francis' speech to the conclave that would later elect him pope, then Cardinal Bergoglio said that the next pope "must be a man who, from the contemplation and adoration of Jesus Christ, helps the Church to go out to the existential peripheries, that helps her to be the fruitful mother, who gains life from 'the sweet and comforting joy of evangelizing.'"[9]

In very similar terms, Archbishop Williams said that the key to preaching the gospel in a completely fresh way is to turn a "self-forgetting gaze towards the light of God in Christ." This purifies not only our hearts but also our vision, so that we may "put on the mind of Christ" and perceive the world as God does, to look at the world from the divine perspective, which is always a gaze of love.

Monks have recognized something very familiar in this approach and feel at home with this emphasis. Gaining a divine perspective in perceiving and interacting with people and the world is the goal of all monastic practices, especially *lectio divina*, the goal of which is a "divine reading" of reality by taking on the mind of God through being soaked in the word of God day after day.

Archbishop Williams said that contemplation is not only the basis for evangelization but is the key to a renewed humanity capable of seeing the world with freedom. "To put it boldly, contemplation is the only ultimate answer to the unreal and insane world that our financial systems and our advertising culture and our chaotic and unexamined emotions encourage us to inhabit."

22. Selling Jesus Short

An important part of the study of Christian theology is the investigation into the great Trinitarian and Christological heresies of the first few centuries. In a strange way, the heresies were a benefit to the Church, because they forced the struggle and ultimately the responses which clarified authentic Christian teaching. The official definitions of that early time have guided the Church ever since.

The Christological heresies fall into two groups: those that minimize Jesus Christ's divinity and those that minimize his humanity. The most prominent example of the denial of the divinity of Christ was the Arian heresy, named after Arius, a Christian preacher from the fourth century. This challenge to orthodoxy prompted the convoking of the first ecumenical council, held at Nicaea in 325. From this council came not only the condemnation of Arianism but the adoption of the Nicene Creed, which is the basis for our creed still recited at Mass on Sundays.

Among the heresies that minimized the humanity of Christ were monophysitism (one nature), which said that Christ has only a single nature, his humanity being absorbed by his divinity, and docetism (to seem), which said that Jesus only seemed to be human, but his physical body was an illusion, and he could not suffer or die. These heresies were condemned by the teaching of the Council of Chalcedon in 451.

Since the time of Chalcedon, the Christian Church has consistently professed, against all challenges, the doctrine of Christ's thorough divinity and thorough humanity: he is truly God and truly man. But that does not mean that in our personal piety or imagination, we might emphasize one over another from time to time.

Commentators have noted that in recent times, it is easier for most Christians to deal with Christ's divinity than with his humanity. We know the human condition and our weaknesses very well, and it is hard to imagine Jesus with the same struggles.

Jesus did not just seem to be a human being like us, going through the motions, but he really was one of us. That is precisely the point. The Letter to the Hebrews is very strong on this: "We do not have a high priest who is unable to sympathize with our weaknesses, but one who has similarly been tested in every way, yet without sin" (4:15). And because we know he understands our situation, we can be confident to approach him. "So let us confidently approach the throne of grace" (4:16). There is one in heaven who understands exactly what we are going through, and therefore . . .

Because Jesus did not sin, we may think he *could* not sin. We may think it an act of reverence to him to give more credit to his divinity than to his humanity. But that would sell him short. A heresy similar to monophysitism was monothelitism (one will), which said Jesus had only one will, a divine will. This was condemned at the Third Council of Constantinople in 680–681. As a human being, Jesus had a free will separate from his divine will. If he had not had a choice in obeying his Father, it would not make sense for him to have prayed in the garden that his Father remove the cup of suffering: "But not what I will but what you will" (Mark 14:36) or to say "I came down from heaven not to do my own will but the will of the one who sent me" (John 6:38). If Jesus had no free human will separate from his divine will, this would have been the kind of "play-acting" taught by docetism.

If we have been accustomed to think that Jesus, because he was the son of God, always knew what he was going to do and did not have to struggle, the realization that his human experience was exactly like ours, except that he didn't sin, may give us a new appreciation of what he went through in becoming flesh for us and redeeming us. More important, it may increase our confidence to share with Jesus our own trials and needs, because he understands our situation personally. The Book of Revelation pictures the risen Jesus "standing in the midst of the throne" as a "Lamb that seemed to have been slain" (5:6), because the resurrection has not blotted out the marks of suffering, though they are now trophies of victory. They are emblematic of the whole human experience of Jesus that is still alive to him.

23. GOD IS THIRSTING FOR ME

St. Augustine was very struck by the story in the fourth chapter of John's Gospel about Jesus meeting with the Samaritan woman at the well. The woman was surprised that Jesus asked her for a drink, since the Jews of the time had nothing to do with Samaritans. St. Augustine is also surprised by Jesus' question but takes the scene to a deeper level. He sees the woman as a symbol of the Church, representing thirsty and needy humanity, and the surprise is that Jesus, the Lord of creation, would ask weak creation for a drink. After all, as Jesus tells the woman, she should instead have asked him for a drink of living water.

The *Catechism* takes the cue from Augustine and sees Christ desiring to meet every human being: "Jesus thirsts; his asking arises from the depths of God's desire for us. Whether we realize it or not, prayer is the encounter of God's thirst with ours. God thirsts that we may thirst for him" (2560). What a breathtaking idea! God is thirsty for a relationship with me! We are very aware that we should seek God, but are we aware that he is seeking us first? The Bible tells us that, but it can be difficult to register. "We love because he first loved us " (1 John 4:19); "God proves his love for us in that while we were still sinners, Christ died for us" (Romans 5:8).

When we pray, we are often hampered and bothered with concerns about getting it right. We don't know what prayers to say, or how long to stay. We are worried about distractions or nodding off. Will our lax performance be more likely to give offense to God rather than praise? The only reason the

Bible gives for postponing prayer is if we are unreconciled with someone (Matthew 5:23-24): it has nothing to do with our feelings of worthiness or our performance. God takes delight in our presence. Our presence is enough. "God thirsts that we may thirst for him" (*Catechism*, 2560). Did you ever see a grandmother frown at an untied shoe as a grandchild leaps into her lap? Most of our doubts and fears about prayer are self-imposed. They come from a confusion about who God is, who we are, and what prayer is all about. God is our loving Father, we are his much-beloved children, and prayer is the way we express our desire for communion with him.

We may be stuck with the childhood image of God as our daily Santa Claus, and still spend our prayer times making our list and checking it twice. Expressing what we would like to have God do for us is part of our prayer relationship with God, but the ordinary pattern is to mature in our relationship with God as we do with people. When we were children we liked to visit certain relatives because of what they gave us; as adults, we visit because of the relationship.

This transition in prayer is beautifully portrayed by the psalmist who prayed to God, "I have stilled my soul, / Like a weaned child to its mother, / weaned is my soul" (Psalm 131:2). A weaned child is one who no longer looks to its mother for milk. Before that, the baby is coming to the mother to get something. A weaned child comes to its mother just to be with mother. We aspire to be weaned away from using God in prayer to loving him. That is what he is thirsting for. "The Christian life consists in continuously scaling the mountain to meet God and then coming back down" (Pope Benedict XVI, Message for Lent 2013, section 3).

Pauline Martin, sister of St. Therese of Lisieux, was the first of five sisters to enter religious life. In a film on the life of St. Therese, Pauline, who was preparing to enter Carmel, is explaining to her younger sisters her excitement: "I must go. Jesus is waiting for me." Sometimes we have an idea of God as stoic, untouched, and unmoved whether we turn away from him or not. That is the God of philosophical abstraction, but not the God of the Bible. The God revealed in the Bible loves us more than a mother (Isaiah 49:15) and, like a loving father worried about his son, paces the floor yearning for him to come home (Hosea 11:1-4). God would give the world for any one of us: "You are precious in my eyes and honored, and I love you" (Isaiah 43:4). This is the God who is thirsting for us, delighting in us, waiting for us. Prayer is where my desire for God meets God's desire for me.

24. HOSEA'S LOVE

The prophet Hosea performed his ministry in the northern kingdom of Israel during the reign of King Jeroboam II in the eighth century BC. It was one of the most prosperous eras in the nation's history, as well as one of the most corrupt. Both Hosea and his contemporary, Amos, preached forcefully against Israel's infidelity, which took the forms of idolatry and oppression of the poor.

Hosea is known as the prophet of God's fidelity toward his chosen people in spite of their infidelity, in both his message and the example of his own life. He married Gomer, who, in their early days together, bore him a daughter and two sons. But she ran away to other lovers, hurting Hosea deeply. God instructed him to take her back, and Hosea did, though it involved public humiliation. He did not punish her but loved her.

The relationship of Hosea and Gomer became, in the preaching of the prophet, the pattern for the relationship of God and his wayward people. The people were faithless, but God remained faithful. He took them back again and again, though the prophetic text pictures God wrestling with himself, at times angry and vindictive, at times patient and forgiving.

Hosea's love for Gomer is the theme of the story he tells, but what emerges from the text is a larger love, the love of Hosea for God and the people of Israel. One of the most beautiful passages in Scripture is the description of God planning how he will lure his wayward people back:

I will allure her now;
    I will lead her into the wilderness
    and speak persuasively to her. . . .
There she will respond as in the days of her youth,
    as on the day she came up from the land of Egypt. . . .
I will betroth you to me forever:
    I will betroth you to me with justice and with judgment,
    with loyalty and with compassion;
I will betroth you to me with fidelity,
    and you shall know the LORD. (Hosea 2:16-17, 21-22)

Where did Hosea get the ability to portray such a tender, loving, and forgiving God, so different from the impersonal and vindictive gods of Israel's neighbors? I think it could only have come from his own intimate relationship with God, his own communion with God in prayer. He speaks as one who knows personally a different God from that imagined by most people of his time.

Perhaps even more striking in this regard is the portrait of God in chapter 11, in which God is pictured as a troubled father, pacing the floor as he talks to himself about his wayward son, Israel.

When Israel was a child I loved him,
    out of Egypt I called my son.
The more I called them,
    the farther they went from me, . . .
I fostered them like those
    who raise an infant to their cheeks;
    I bent down to feed them. (Hosea 11:1-2, 4)

God then becomes heated as he remembers the infidelity of his son. He will make him pay:

> He shall return to the land of Egypt,
>> Assyria shall be his king,
>> because they have refused to repent.
> The sword shall rage in his cities: . . .
>> though [my people] call on God in unison,
>> he shall not raise them up. (Hosea 11:5-6, 7)

But he can't do it:

> How could I give you up, Ephraim,
>> or deliver you up, Israel? . . .
> My heart is overwhelmed,
>> my pity is stirred.
> I will not give vent to my blazing anger,
>> I will not destroy Ephraim again;
> For I am God and not a man,
>> the Holy One present among you. (Hosea 11:8-9)

God's love for his people is so strong that he cannot let them go, no matter how often they have betrayed his love. He sees them frightened, trembling like doves, and his heart goes out to them, overcoming his anger: "I will resettle them in their homes, / oracle of the LORD" (Hosesa 11:11).

Where did Hosea get such an intimate image of God, so tender, so faithful, so forgiving, so unlike the images of God in his culture and environment? I think it is because he did not know about God only "by hearsay" (Job 42:5), but he came to know and love God personally and to be convinced, from God's tenderness and mercy in his own life, of God's unyielding love for the wayward chosen people. ∾

One of my favorite Bible verses, Psalm 72:20, is almost never quoted. It is part of a psalm, but when the rest of the psalm is published in prayer books, even in official prayer texts of the Church, the verse is regularly omitted. It isn't scandalous or obscure, but as soon as you read it you will understand why it is often left out: "The end of the psalms of David, son of Jesse." The sentence is an editorial remark.

There are many editorial comments in the Bible that were added to texts—for example, the instructions at the beginning of some of the psalms, added when they were compiled for use in worship. The introduction to Psalm 6, for instance, has the note: "With stringed instruments, 'upon the eighth'" (6:1). No one any longer knows what was meant by "upon the eighth." It was probably some kind of musical key. The same is true of "upon the *gittith*" and "according to *Muth Labben*," the opening lines of Psalms 8 and 9, respectively.

Why do I like the particular editorial remark in Psalm 72:20? Evidently, I am not struck by the verse's poetry or any depth of meaning. What appeals to me is its off-camera character and its exposure of an unintended message—unintended, that is, by its human author. The editorial instruction was not planned for inclusion in the published text, but it entered into the biblical canon because later scribes, respectful of the sacredness of the Bible, did not feel it was within their competence to omit it. Now the verse is part of the inspired text, and the Bible has captured in it a familiar quirk of human nature that is still alive and recognizable many centuries later.

Psalms is one of the biblical books that took centuries to compile. The various stages have left their mark in the present text, which contains five sections, or "books," clearly distinguished in most modern translations. These books begin at Psalms 1, 42, 73, 90, and 107, each ending with a doxology or hymn of praise to God, such as at the end of the third book: "Blessed be the LORD forever! Amen and amen!" (Psalm 89:53).

The First Book of the Psalms (1-41) is the earliest collection, probably put together during the Babylonian Exile (BC 587–538) in order to preserve what was in danger of being lost. Thirty-seven of these forty-one psalms are identified in the title as psalms of David. No other author is named. After the exile, a few generations later, a group of Temple musicians called the "Sons of Korah" began adding a few of their psalms to the collection of what was eventually to become the Second Book (Psalms 42-72), containing also psalms attributed to Asaph (Psalm 50) and Solomon (Psalm 72), as well as eighteen more psalms of David.

At this point, the individual or group responsible for the collection of psalms evidently felt that the process was getting out of hand and that it was time to close the book and protect the traditional collection. Younger singers were adding their music, and because the editor or editors just didn't know where it might end up, that is when he or they bundled up the two books of psalms and published them with the instruction I like so much: "The end of the psalms of David, son of Jesse."

But they were not ended. Years later, another Davidic psalm was found, and it was published with the new psalms of the two other groups, probably choir guilds, already represented in the second book, the Asaph group (eleven psalms, 73-83) and the Korah group (four psalms, 84-85, 87-88), plus a psalm attributed to Ethan the Ezrahite (Psalm 89) to make a third book (73-89). Surely that would do it. Now the psalms of David are certainly ended. But no, later a fourth book (90-106) included two more Davidic psalms, and finally a fifth book (107-150) was published with not just one or two but fifteen more psalms of David! The Holy Spirit was obviously not finished with the "psalms of David" as early as some would have liked. The collection did not stop with 72 psalms but grew to the grand total of 150.

But there at the end of Psalm 72, we have a window into an ancient editorial debate. Someone was trying to put the lid on early: possibly someone worried about opening the Temple up to the new music, or just the opposite, someone felt the Davidic psalms were by now too old-fashioned. Whatever the reason, it wasn't time to end the Psalter, and the instruction to do so looks funny halfway through the book.

We all look funny or silly or sad putting our foot down when the discussion isn't over. Maybe I'm fascinated by this verse because I see myself in it. ❦

26. TIMELESSNESS
IN OUR HEARTS

Nowhere in Scripture is the tension that human beings experience as citizens of time and eternity better captured than in the Book of Ecclesiastes: "God has made everything appropriate to its time, but has put the timeless into their hearts so they cannot find out, from beginning to end, the work which God has done" (3:11).

As soon as humans grow past early infancy, the passage of time impresses itself constantly, as well as the awareness of "times," the perception that certain events or experiences belong to particular hours and days and seasons of both nature and of human life. It is this reality that begins the meditation in Ecclesiastes 3: "There is . . . /A time to give birth, and a time to die" (3:1, 2). This is God's doing: "[He] has made everything appropriate to its time" (3:11).

Because we understand the passage of time and can interpret times, humans may think that this awareness gives us the ability to grasp the whole of existence and the meaning of it all. Through the centuries, many people have thought they could figure it out and have imposed various interpretations on reality as a key to the whole, but all of them are ultimately unsatisfactory because there is always data that cannot be covered by their big blankets. The meaning of what God has done "from beginning to end" is beyond us (Ecclesiastes 3:11).

Some get closer than others, as is the insight of T. S. Eliot in "The Dry Salvages":

Men's curiosity searches past and future
And clings to that dimension. But to apprehend
The point of intersection of the timeless
With time, is an occupation for the saint—
No occupation either, but something given
And taken, in a lifetime's death in love,
Ardour and selflessness and self-surrender. . . .
For most of us, there is only the unattended
Moment, the moment in and out of time. (lines 591-599)

The saints get closer because they get closer to God. It is "something given," not earned or learned (line 595).

What has put the meaning of it all perpetually beyond our fingertips is this: God "has put the timeless into their hearts" (Ecclesiastes 3:11). The word translated "timeless" is the Hebrew word usually translated "eternity" (*ha'olam*) and here means a consciousness that there is something beyond the present, something that holds it all together but transcends human perception.

God has made everything right in its time, a time for this and a time for that. "I recognized that whatever God does will endure forever; there is no adding to it, or taking from it" (Ecclesiastes 3:14). We can appreciate everything we see in this life, and we can understand much of it, especially as it comes to us in parts and pieces, but we cannot expect to understand how it all fits together. He "has put the timeless into [our] hearts," so that none of the individual events and experiences of this world are completely self-contained

(3:11). We are haunted by the sense of a larger design that is beyond our grasp.

This may seem to doom us to futility, and many have taken that road, or it may be the very thing that gives us hope. We human beings experience within us an awareness of a reality beyond that keeps us perpetually dissatisfied and yearning for something more. Of all the myriad species of creatures on earth, only human beings have this inner awareness of eternity, so it certainly isn't necessary for earthly existence. But all human beings have it, so it has to be by design. And if by design, there has to be a designer, as timeless as the timelessness that has been put into our hearts.

All earthly creatures have life, but humans, at no extra charge, carry within themselves the signature of the Creator.

27. Humility and Truth

On September 19, 2010, Pope Benedict XVI beatified Cardinal John Henry Newman in Birmingham, England, where Newman had spent almost all of his years since 1845, when he became a Catholic, until his death in 1890 at age 89. It was the appropriate location for this pronouncement, since it was at Birmingham that Newman was beatified.

Newman is known for many things: his leadership of the Oxford Movement in the Anglican Church in the 1830s and 1840s; his theological and spiritual influence through his many writings as an Anglican and as a Catholic, many of which are still in print today; his personal influence in the spiritual journeys of countless people during his lifetime and since; and the clarity and beauty of his English prose. Many other accomplishments could be added. But it wasn't because of any of these that he was beatified. He could have been a saint without any of it, or he could have been a reprobate with all of it. He was beatified because, through much struggle over a long life, he was able to turn all of this over to God and put his whole life at God's service.

With his towering intellect, Newman entered this world with a great advantage. He could have been whatever he wanted to be. But his gifts were no special advantage for the ultimate purpose of existence: eternal life in the permanent world of the kingdom of God. All of us have the same chance at that, no matter our gifts. In a sense, Newman's brilliant gifts made it more difficult. We know what Jesus said about the special hazard of riches for entering the kingdom of God: "It is easier for a camel to pass through the eye of a needle" (Matthew 19:24).

Newman knew he was rich, and he knew the hazard. He was very aware of the dangers of pride and self-sufficiency, and he knew that his only chance was to serve God in radical humility. But how, for a man with his gifts? His insight was to seek and follow the truth, wherever it led him, with undeviating fidelity. This is impossible to do without humility. The proud person is always right, always presuming to know the truth. Newman had very strong opinions and good reasons for them, but he was always bending his will to submission to the truth as he discovered it, which is ultimately the Truth, God himself. One of his well-known sayings is this: "To grow is to change, and to be perfect means to have changed often."[10] This willingness to follow his conscience is what led him to become a Catholic at the height of his position and influence in the Anglican Church, and to start over on the bottom rung.

I said earlier that it was at Birmingham that Newman became a saint. That is a conjecture, of course, about something only God knows. Newman was well on his sainthood journey as an Anglican before he came to Birmingham, but he had a long way and many years to go, and he could have turned away from the sainthood path at any time. It was in his years as a Catholic, mostly hidden years, that, unexpectedly, he found the greatest challenge to his humble search for the truth.

The years from 1845 to 1879 were the years of the victory of humility in his life, the time he was passing through the needle's eye, doing his work patiently in the shadow of jealousy and intrigue, and overcoming the temptation to strike back, which he might have done with withering power. He stayed the course, seeking strength and solace silently, in his hidden prayer and his mostly hidden work.

It is this victory of grace, validated for the Church recently by a healing miracle that is being celebrated in his beatification. He gives the Church the witness of a man of recent history with premier human endowments, thoroughly modern and aware of everything going on around him and of the privileges he could command, focusing on the "one thing" and humbling himself to serve God and the people sent his way, seeking only the truth (Luke 10:42).

An oft-quoted reflection of Newman, written in his early years to describe the search for and submission to the truth as a plan of life, can now be taken as autobiographical of Newman, and can also be utilized as a plan of life for each of us:

Truth bears witness by itself to its Divine Author. He who obeys God conscientiously, and lives holily, forces all about him to believe and tremble before the unseen power of Christ. To the world indeed at large he witnesses not; for few can see him near enough to be moved by his manner of living. But to his neighbours he manifests the Truth in proportion to their knowledge of him; and some of them, through God's blessing, catch the holy flame, cherish it, and in their turn transmit it. And thus in a dark world Truth still makes way in spite of the darkness, passing from hand to hand." (*The Works of Cardinal Newman*, 292-293)

PART V

PLACING YOUR HOPE IN GOD

28. Fear of the Lord

A number of biblical texts encourage the fear of the Lord, and the tone of these texts is invariably positive: the fear of the Lord is a "treasure" (Isaiah 33:6) and "the beginning of wisdom" (Psalms 111:10); "the fear of the LORD leads to life" (Proverbs 19:23); and "the angel of the LORD encamps / around those who fear" the Lord (Psalms 34:8). But we don't sense that kind of language being very encouraging. What does the Bible mean by fear?

There are also passages that encourage us not to fear: "Do not be afraid, Mary, for you have found favor with God" (Luke 1:30). God told Abraham, our father, "Do not fear, Abram! I am your shield" (Genesis 15:1). It is typical that God or his messenger gives the reassurance: "Do not be afraid" (1 Kings 17:13), especially, "Do not fear, for I am with you" (Genesis 26:24) and "Do not fear: I am with you; / do not be anxious: I am your God" (Isaiah 41:10).

So the Bible must be talking about two kinds of fear. This is expressd graphically in Moses' instruction to the people after the giving of the Ten Commandments at Sinai: "Do not be afraid, for God has come only to test you and put the fear of him upon you so you do not sin" (Exodus 20:20). The people are told not to be afraid in order that they may fear! Don't fear or do fear, which is it? The reason for our quandary comes from the limitations of language. The word "fear" may mean to be afraid and even seriously so, "cringing fear," or it may mean to have reverence and respect. Those are two quite different concepts

113

and experiences. When the Bible tells us to fear not so that we may fear the Lord, it is saying do not be afraid in order that you may have reverence, because what is called "cringing fear" makes it impossible to have reverence, which requires confidence in the other.

Ultimately, to fear God in the sense encouraged in those difficult Scripture passages simply means to put God first. We listen to and act upon many suggestions during a typical day. Some we disregard because they are not to the point, others because we don't have confidence in their source. When we accept a suggestion, it is a sign we respect the source, and at that moment, in a biblical sense, we "fear" that person. We are not afraid of him or her, but we have enough respect and confidence to follow the person's suggestion. If what we are urged to do is good, that person has led us in the right way, and we are still walking in the fear of God.

On the other hand, when we follow another person's suggestion or example to do something we know is wrong, at that moment we fear that person more than we fear God. We have put someone else before God. When we have lost this fear of God is when we should truly be afraid.

Today there are many voices vying for our attention—on TV, through the Internet, through smartphones, in papers, and in magazines. We are bombarded with messages, and perhaps we are tempted to follow the wrong path. The voice of Jesus breaks through: "Do not be afraid. I am with you. Put your trust in me." If we respond to this summons and refocus our faith and commitment, we profess again that God is first in our lives and that we want to live by his truth. When we do this, we are putting God first, and living by the fear of the Lord.

Fear of God is not scary. It provides the safest and surest way to live. Simply put God first in your life, and you will be at peace. But that doesn't mean there won't be a struggle. There may be people in your world who don't want you to fear God. Jesus tells us, "Do not be afraid of those who kill the body but after that can do no more" (Luke 12:4). No more! What more is there to do? Jesus goes on, "I shall show you whom to fear. Be afraid of the one who after killing has the power to cast into Genenna" (12:5). Be afraid of those people, but don't fear them. Fear God. ❧

29. Free from Fear

Every morning, members of the Church throughout the world pray the Canticle of Zechariah, the *Benedictus*, praising God for the gift of salvation in Christ that was signaled in the birth of Zechariah's son, John the Baptist: "Blessed be the Lord, the God of Israel, / for he has visited and brought redemption to his people" (Luke 1:68). God has saved us "from the hand of enemies," so that "without fear we might worship him in holiness and righteousness / before him all our days" (1:74-75).

We might wonder who the enemies are and what is the fear. Illumination is provided by a passage in the Letter to the Hebrews that says that by his death, Jesus "destroy[ed] the one who has the power of death, that is, the devil," in order to "free those who through fear of death had been subject to slavery all their life" (Hebrews 2:14, 15). These are strong words. How does fear of death make us slaves? The letter isn't speaking here of the natural fear of death that we all have, which has its good side in making us alert to danger and encouraging us to take care of the life God has given us.

The fear of death in this biblical passage has a deeper meaning. It means fear of the emptiness and darkness that come with annihilation, the fear of ceasing to exist as a person. An animal cannot experience this fear of death, but only an intelligent being with self-awareness and the ability to think about the future. Jesus Christ, by destroying the power of this ultimate death, has freed us from the inner slavery that makes us live without hope. Now we can face danger, disease, and even physical death with interior freedom, confident that our real life cannot be destroyed, and we will live on.

Part of this fear of ultimate death is the fear of being eternally alone, not counting or not relating. The beauty of Christ's victory over death is that as we pass to life beyond this world, we continue in relation to those we have known in this life, both those who have already died and those who are still living. Those of us who are still in this life are supported by the knowledge that we are still in communion with those who have gone before us.

For those still bound by the slavery of this ultimate fear, we are terribly insecure and doomed to devoting all our energy to building the barricades and locking the doors. No matter how secure we become on the outside by amassing money, property, or power, until we are free from the fear of death, we will always be insecure interiorly.

There are legitimate forms of insurance for protection of life, health, and property, but without interior freedom, an exaggerated drive for security can destroy the most important things we want to protect: our relationships, our values, and even our faith. "Those who enjoy life most," said Pope Francis in The Joy of the Gospel, "are those who leave security on the shore and become excited by the mission of communicating life to others" (section 10). But the self-protection that comes with the fear of death creates suspicion, causing us to see others as obstacles, and rather than communicating life, it is "death-dealing" (in our time leading ever more to the toleration of abortion and euthanasia), and robs us of all joy and peace.

Jesus has liberated us from this slavery and offered us the freedom of the children of God. The wonderful peace this brings is described poetically at the end of the *Benedictus*, which can set the tone as we begin the day:

Because of the tender mercy of our God
  by which the daybreak from on high will visit us
to shine on those who sit in darkness and death's shadow,
to guide our feet into the path of peace. (Luke 1:78-79)

30. The Gospel of the Poor

In February 2000, I attended a meeting of North and Central American Benedictine men and women superiors in Mexico City. I had responded to an invitation from Benedictine sisters in Cuernavaca, fifty miles south of the capital, to arrive a few days early to join them in their ministry to the poor.

There is a section of dwellings in the center of Cuernavaca called La Estación (the Station) because it is located in the midst of the former network of railroad tracks that had been a hub of transportation in years past. Mexican peasants tried to escape their dire poverty by saving their money to come to the city, hoping for a better way of life. There weren't enough jobs to go around, of course, so many of the new arrivals ended up settling down in the vicinity of the train station, eventually 40,000 of them, living in equal or worse poverty than before, in huts nailed together from scrap wood and tin.

The city government could not handle the influx and tried various ways to discourage the relocation, ultimately discontinuing train service at that location and cutting off electricity and other services. Through ingenuity, these new inhabitants found ways to survive in a difficult environment. To my surprise, the first request to me was not for money but for the soft drink bottle cap I was about to throw away. The aluminum caps were precious because they could be used at connection points in their construction where nails driven through them would not rust.

My most vivid memory of the visit to the Station was of an elderly crippled woman. Carmen had lost her husband but learned to embroider and enlisted her grandson to sell pieces of her work on the street for money to buy food. A few weeks before we arrived, she had fallen and broken her hand, upon which she depended for her livelihood. Yet there she was, propping herself on one leg at the door of her hut, beaming and holding out to us with her good hand a plastic bag containing three eggs and half a head of lettuce, which was all the food she had. We could not take her food, but we did stay to hear her story, which was interjected frequently with the exclamation, "*Gracias a Diós!*" or "Thanks be to God!" Carmen shared stories of hardships that still praised God, saying, "I lost my husband, but *gracias a Diós*, I learned to embroider"; "I broke my hand, but *gracias a Diós*, I still have one good one"; and "I don't have much to eat, but *gracias a Diós*, people have been sharing with me."

In his encyclical The Joy of the Gospel, Pope Francis said, "[The poor] have much to teach us. . . . In their difficulties they know the suffering Christ. We need to let ourselves be evangelized by them . . . and to embrace the mysterious wisdom which God wishes to share with us through them" (§ 198).

What all of us need to learn from Carmen—and what we desperately want to know—is what the source of her hope and joy is. Billions of dollars are spent in our country every day to bring ease, comfort, and pleasure, or what is, in general terms, called happiness. All of these things are fleeting and may be taken from our lives at any moment by sickness, accident, job termination, or similar unforeseen circumstances.

What Carmen had was something permanent, something that is not for sale and cannot be bought. She had joy, a hidden source within a person that gives meaning to everything in life and cannot be taken away. We may give it up or give it away, but it cannot be taken away. Not only the poor, certainly not all the poor, have this inner joy. Many of those blessed with the world's goods have it too, but its source is not so clear as in those who seem to have no reason for joy.

Carmen's joy, overcoming all external problems, sprang from inside her and, as her words made clear, was inspired by faith, her confidence in God's promises and his love for her. Nothing in her external circumstances could take this away. In fact, she possessed her joy so completely—or it possessed her—that she was able to give it away without exhausting any of it in herself. Like the widow in Mark's Gospel, she, "from her poverty, has contributed all she had, her whole livelihood" (Mark 12:44), and those who met her were enriched.

31. Purity of Heart

In the short chapter on prayer in his monastic *Rule*, St. Benedict has this admonition: "We should realize that it is not in much talking that we shall be heard, but in purity of heart and tearful compunction" (20:3). In mentioning "purity of heart," Benedict is connecting to a mother lode of early monastic spirituality. Its biblical source is Jesus' beatitude "Blessed are the clean of heart, / for they will see God" (Matthew 5:8) and the tradition expressed in Psalm 24: "Who may go up the mountain of the LORD? / Who can stand in his holy place? / 'The clean of hand and pure of heart'" (3-4).

We may be conditioned to think of "purity of heart" in terms of sexual purity, and while this is part of it, it is but only a sliver. St. Benedict took over the term from John Cassian, who a century earlier had synthesized the ancient monastic spirituality in his *Institutes* and *Conferences*. For Cassian, purity of heart is the goal of monastic life, bringing freedom from the domination of sinful passions, resulting in inner peace. It is not a goal we can reach on our own, but only with the help of the grace that draws us toward God.

In the 1840s, Sören Kierkegaard wrote *Purity of Heart Is to Will One Thing*, in which he explains, "In truth to will one thing, then, can only mean to will the Good, because every other object is not a unity; and the will that only wills that object, therefore, must become double-minded" (3:1). With that last word—double-minded—we encounter a term in the spiritual tradition that identifies the opposite of purity of heart. The Letter of James admonishes, "Cleanse your hands, you sinners, and purify your hearts, you of two minds" (4:8). Earlier, this letter described the double-minded person as shaky in faith and "unstable in all his ways" (1:8). This isn't the same as duplicity, which is purposeful deceit, nor like being torn between decisions, such as whether to stay with a present job or seek a new one, or whether to change majors. It isn't even parallel to St. Paul's dilemma: "I do not do what I want, but I do what I hate" (Romans 7:15). Paul has no doubt what he wants to do; he just finds himself betraying that desire by his actions. We all know this struggle. More to the point in understanding "double-minded" is what Jesus says in the Sermon on the Mount about serving two masters: "You cannot serve God and mammon" (Matthew 6:24). This is being double-minded in the sense of Kierkegaard or James: not having decided among masters which to serve, not having a clear dedication to a single goal, and going through life without realizing it. Jesus chose the example of God and mammon probably because failing to decide which of those claimants is the real master is such a common trap.

We may find ourselves double-minded in a much subtler way. The late Cardinal Joseph Bernardin told the story of a major conversion that took place in his life during the time he was Archbishop of Cincinnati (1972–1982). While he was at dinner with three younger diocesan priests, they challenged him that he was not sufficiently focused on his spiritual life, not a real man of prayer. At first, he was shocked and even insulted by their remarks, but the more he thought about it, the more he realized that they were right. He was so busy with the many demands of the archdiocese that he was not giving priority to prayer. He said that he realized that he was focused on the Church rather than on Christ. He dedicated himself from then on to the task of a holy hour of prayer every day, no matter how busy, tired, or distracted he might be. This dedication to prayer, he said, changed his life.

"Focused on the Church" doesn't sound so bad. There are lots of worse things to focus on. But even the Church, with its activities and structures, may distract us from the one thing necessary. As St. John of the Cross noted, "God does not fit in an occupied heart."[11]

In his intimate conversation with God in the *Confessions*, St. Augustine wrote, "You have made us for yourself, O Lord, and our heart is restless until it rests in you."[12] Nothing else will suffice; nothing else will satisfy. Purify our hearts, O Lord, and heal our double minds.

32. Within Your Wounds Hide Me

The Anima Christi is a traditional after-Mass prayer by an unknown author of the early fourteenth century. It has been a favorite since it first appeared and is still printed in the Roman Missal. The prayer is not as well-known now as it was in the days of the Latin Mass, when it was printed in the personal daily missals that were needed for the vernacular translation. However, it is still available on prayer cards and remains popular with many Catholics. The name comes from the first invocation of the prayer, "Soul of Christ."

> Soul of Christ, sanctify me.
> Body of Christ, save me.
> Blood of Christ, inebriate me.
> Water from the side of Christ, wash me.
> Passion of Christ, strengthen me.
> O good Jesus, hear me.
> Within your wounds conceal me.
> Do not permit me to be parted from you.
> From the evil for protect me.
> In the hour of my death call me.
> And bid me come to you, to praise you with all your
> saints for ever and ever. Amen.

The first half of the prayer is rich in Eucharistic themes, which has made the prayer ideal for post-communion reflection. I am struck by the seventh line, which brings something new and unexpected: "Within your wounds conceal me." The prayer is directed to the living Christ, who is now the Christ in glory, and every part of his human nature is transformed. His wounds are glorious now, but they are still there. They are not obliterated by the transforming light of the resurrection. This same point is made vividly in the Book of Revelation, where the risen Jesus appears "standing in the midst of the throne" as a "Lamb that seemed to have been slain" (5:6) at the throne of God. He still has the wounds of Calvary, but now they are trophies of victory. But their continuing presence in the body of the Lamb also makes the statement that Jesus is still one of us and still knows what human suffering is.

This is a very important corollary of the gift of the Incarnation. Jesus became one of us, thoroughly human, "emptied himself" (Philippians 2:7), was born in Bethlehem, grew up in Nazareth, preaching and healing throughout the country-side, and being crucified in Jerusalem. All of this limitation was overcome in the resurrection, but what Jesus underwent in his human body was not obliterated. His human experience lives forever in the glorified Jesus. This gives us the kind of access spoken about in the Letter to the Hebrews:

> Since we have a great high priest who has passed through the heavens, Jesus, the Son of God, let us hold fast to our confession. For we do not have a high priest who is unable to sympathize with our weaknesses, but one who has similarly been tested in every way, yet without sin. So let us confidently approach the throne of grace to receive mercy and to find grace for timely help. (Hebrews 4:14-16)

When all is lost and there is nowhere else to turn, we can turn to the One who understands our suffering.

There are times when no words are adequate, when no sympathy gives comfort, and when all we need is a safe place to hide. We have experienced rejection, betrayal, or devastating abuse, or we have betrayed what we were living for. We may have seen something so horrible that momentarily we cannot go on. "Within your wounds conceal me" (Anima Christi). We need no reasoning and no promise that it will get better; we need a place to hide and be loved. Jesus' wounds are not only transformed, but they are transforming. Now and for all eternity, they will be healing wounds. When the time comes, when life comes crushing down, they are a place to hide. ❧

Endnotes

1. "Pray Always since Prayer Expands Desire - Augustine." *Crossroads Initiative*, October 24, 2017. https://www.crossroadsinitiative.com/media/articles/prayer-expands-desire/

2. "2247 Prayer." *Augnet*. Accessed April 17, 2018. http://www.augnet.org/en/works-of-augustine/his-spiritual-tradition/2247-prayer/.

3. "A Quote by T.S. Eliot." *Goodreads*. Accessed April 17, 2018. https://www.goodreads.com/quotes/145500-for-us-there-is-only-the-trying-the-rest-is.

4. "Full Text of Selected Letters of Saint Jane Frances De Chantal." Accessed April 17, 2018. https://archive.org/stream/selectedletterso00chanuoft/selectedletterso00chanuoft_djvu.txt

5. "God or the Works of God?" *The Abby Message*, Vol LXX, No. 4. Accessed April 17, 2018. http://www.countrymonks.org/documents/2014/11/TAM_Spring_14_webcopy.pdf

6. Southwell, Robert. "I Dye Alive." *Bartleby*. Accessed May 2, 2018. http://www.bartleby.com/236/4.html

7. "Our Daily Bread." *St. Mary of the Valley*. Accessed May 2, 2018. http://stmaryvalleybloom.org/homily-body-christ-c.html

8. "St. Augustine: Sermon on the Mount; Harmony of the Gospels; Homilies on the Gospels." *Christian Classics Ethereal Library*. Accessed May 2, 2018. http://www.ccel.org/ccel/schaff/npnf106.v.iii.vii.html

9. "The 4-Minute Speech That Got Pope Francis Elected?" *Catholic Answers*. Accessed May 2, 2018. https://www.catholic.com/magazine/online-edition/the-4-minute-speech-that-got-pope-francis-elected.

10. McNamara, Pat. "Newman's Road to Rome." *Catholic Education Resource Center*. Accessed May 2, 2018. https://www.catholiceducation.org/en/faith-and-character/faith-and-character/newman-s-road-to-rome.html

11. "Wisdom of Carmel." *Mount Carmel*. Accessed May 2, 2018. https://srhelena.blogspot.com/p/sayings-of-love-light.html

12. "Our Heart Is Restless Until It Rests in You - Augustine." *Crossroads Initiative*. October 28, 2017. https://www.crossroadsinitiative.com/media/articles/ourheartisrestlessuntilitrestsinyou/

the WORD among us ®

The *Spirit* of Catholic Living

This book was published by The Word Among Us. Since 1981, The Word Among Us has been answering the call of the Second Vatican Council to help Catholic laypeople encounter Christ in the Scriptures.

The name of our company comes from the prologue to the Gospel of John and reflects the vision and purpose of all of our publications: to be an instrument of the Spirit, whose desire is to manifest Jesus' presence in and to the children of God. In this way, we hope to contribute to the Church's ongoing mission of proclaiming the gospel to the world so that all people would know the love and mercy of our Lord and grow more deeply in their faith as missionary disciples.

Our monthly devotional magazine, *The Word Among Us*, features meditations on the daily and Sunday Mass readings, and currently reaches more than one million Catholics in North America and another half million Catholics in one hundred countries around the world. Our book division, The Word Among Us Press, publishes numerous books, Bible studies, and pamphlets that help Catholics grow in their faith.

To learn more about who we are and what we publish, log on to our website at www.wau.org. There you will find a variety of Catholic resources that will help you grow in your faith.

Embrace His Word, Listen to God . . .

www.wau.org